The Book of Joe

THE BOOK OF
JOE

IAN ROSS

Cover design by Terry Gallagher/Doowah Design Inc.
Cover photograph by Debra Mosher
Printed and bound in Canada

Published with the financial assistance of the Manitoba Arts Council and The
Canada Council for the Arts.

Royalties from the sales of this book are being donated to support theatre in
Manitoba.

Canadian Cataloguing in Publication Data

Ross, Ian, 1968–
    The book of Joe

ISBN 1-896239-59-5
    I. Title.
PS8585.O84014B66 1999   081   C99-901529-X
PR9199.3.R68   1999

To my love, and friend, Debra

Table of Contents

Author's Ramblings & More Thank-You's

Wow. That's the word that best describes what's happened and how I feel about doing *Joe from Winnipeg*. As I've said many times before, writing and performing Joe is a great honour to me. I'm not exactly sure how much of an effect (if any) I have, but that's a good thing. I'm sure if I found out I would either stop doing Joe or think it was a little more important than it should be. I'm just glad people like hearing what he has to say. It's been fun seeing how the character has evolved. It hasn't become any easier, but he does speak a little differently, as some of you may notice in this book. Hey, by the way, thanks for buying it. I and the people it supports appreciate it. Because the last book did well, my publisher told me that maybe some day we'd do another Joe book. So…I organized the Joe's a little better. I even dated them. So putting this book together wasn't quite like reassembling dino DNA. It was more like putting recipes in order. My thanks to my wife, Debra, Cecil Rosner, Kim Dopheide and my producer Tom Anniko (the proverbial person without whom none of this would have been possible). Thanks to you listeners and readers and everyone who allow me to come into your homes. Meegwetch.

Mouses

Hey you guys, this is me, Joe from Winnipeg. Today I'm gonna be talkin' to you 'bout mouses. I almos said "meeses" eh, like Jinx da Cat. He hates the meeses to pieces. Boy me too. Sort of. So anyways, boy it's good to get my big mouth back on the radio here. I missed talkin' to you guys. I was drivin' my fam'ly crazy. Always commentatin' on stuff. Hey how 'bout dat Clinton and Monica. What's up with that? I'd say. An how 'bout the stocks markets? What's up with that? An the Russian thing? What's… You get the idea. Boy dey did too eh? Tellin' me to go bug somebody else. So here I am. Anyways, mouses. So I was watchin' da win move the trees the other day eh. Sittin' der eatin' a choclate bar. An den I hear dis funny noise. "Chick a chick a chick a chick". Boy, I looked at my bar to see if I was eatin' the wrappin' again eh. But I wasn't. So I sat der an watched a little more. Da leaves were makin' dat soun, like, "See ya. Be back nex year." I know some of yous is wondrin' why I'm watchin' the win eh? I figured it was time I do more Native type stuff. So anyways, den I hear this "chick a chick a chick a chick" soun again eh. Boy, dis time I wait. An den I listen to hear where dat "chick a chick a chick" comin' from. An I look, an I see dis other choclate bar I dropped on the floor from before eh. Boy. An der was a mouse eatin' it. I jumped up from my chair 'cause I was so shock eh. Boy, den I wen into cat mode right away. I crouch behine my chair an I watched dat choclate. Den I get dis funny feelin' eh. An I turn my head an look by the rad e ator an der's dis little grey head peekin' out an lookin' at me. Boy, I jumped again. An dat mouse took off. But in dat momen our eyes met. I knew it was war eh. So I wen an grabbed a shoe. An I sat by the door waitin' for him, 'cause dat was his only escape. An after sittin' der for about two hours an tinkin' bad tings like, Who do I know's got a gun eh? I wen to go ask my frien Laughin' Louie. Dey call him dat 'cause he laughs all the time eh. Myself, I can't tink of a better nickname to have. So I ask Louie, how do I get rid of dis mouse in da house eh. An he says to me, "You got a hammer?" An I says, "Yeah." An he says, "Can I borrow it?" "What for?" I says to him. "So I can nail someting," he says to me an den he laughs. An den he tells me to jus put out traps. So I did. An I even used dat choclate he was eatin'. Sure enough nex morning dat choclate was gone an dose traps was unset eh. So den I heard put peanut butter on der. So I tried dat. An I could swear eh, dat dat little mouse lef me a note wantin' some jam, too. Boy, by dis time I was so frustrated. An den I figured it out 'bout dis little mouse. He's jus like us eh. Tryin' to make a livin'. Tryin' to get by. I even figured dat I didn't really wanna kill him. Dat was jus me tryin' to be macho. Or do what I always heard you're s'posed to do. Da best ting would be to trap him an throw him in a field somewhere eh. Or else give him a 'viction notice. Dis one's so smart I bet he can read. So I'm gonna leave him alone for now. He's been doin' dat for me. He's even been doin' his busness where I can't see it eh. So I guess dat's what I'm sayin' to yous, is dat when yer tryin' to get by today, do yer bes to avoid da dummies like me, holdin' der shoes over der head. An dat even dey aren't all bad. Sometimes we all get a little obsessed, eh. Look at dat old Ken Starr. What's up with that? If him an me was after dat mouse we would've blowed up da house by now. This is Joe from Winnipeg. Meegwetch.

Runnin'

Hey you guys, this is me, Joe from Winnipeg. Today I'm gonna be talkin' to you 'bout all kines of runnin'. So. You guys ever woner what happens to dat stuff at the bottom of the toaser? I did. DO NOT. I say dat again. DO NOT STICK FORKS IN DER. 'Specially with da toaser plugged in. Make sure you take yer toaser to a toaser cleanin' professional. I took mine to my mechanic frien, Brian. He jus shot it with some compress air eh? Boy, dose toas crumbs were stickin' to all da grease like everything. But at leas it smelled good. Anyways, so my frien Leslee asked me, "Joe. How come my toilet keeps runnin'?" I jus wanted to say to her, "Is it runnin' right now?" An she'd say, "Yeah." An I'd say, "Well. You better go catch it den." Boy, an we'd laugh. Or not. I decided agains dat eh. 'Cause I figure it's not up to da high stanard of quality comedy I genrally provide her with eh. All I could say was, "Maybe it's got to do with dat ting dat looks like a marshmallow on a stick. 'Cept it's floatin' in da back of yer toilet. Or else maybe it jus wants some attention. I doan know." But she got me tinkin' eh. I should be like dat toilet. Do more runnin'. Do some good for myself. Nahh. Den I got it. I wish I could say dat I heard voices like da Joan of Arc. Or else I saw a light an got a message. But all I could tink was, runnin'. Toilet. Runnin'. Toilet. Mayor race. Winnipeg. Boy, eh. Go runnin' for da mayor race. Actually it had more to do with wantin' to make toilets better for my friens. An all the citizens of Winnipeg. But I'm gettin' too literal here. An I better save my toilet speech for later in da campaign. So I said to myself, "Self, what would you do if you runned for mayor?" Haven you always wanted to be called Yer Worship. People could say, "'scuse me Joe yer worship." Waarns. I'm jus kiddin' 'bout dat. But I did figure it's someting you doan really need experience for eh. Well you do, but you doan have to have it to run for da job. An I'd even get a pair of dose big scissors to cut ribbons with. Maybe even a nice hat dat said "Mayor" on der. An den I thought, what would you do? Well. I guess I'd make the Portage Avenue wider again, downtown. What's up with dat eh? Have you guys seen the rush hour down there? Tree lanes. Or else maybe I'd findly get dat monorail put in. I doan know. All I do know is dat it's hard bein' a leader eh. Dey got to work for us an us for dem a little bit too. I love my city. An even all da other cities an towns. An my province. Da one ting I'd try do if I was da mayor is make our communities better places eh. I hope dat's what all da candidates want. You know what else? I figure if I could be da mayor, you could too eh? We could all be the leader in our own ways. Boy, dat would be good. An den maybe even somebody could help fix my frien Leslee's toilet. I'm Joe from Winnipeg. Meegwetch.

NSF

Hey you guys, this is me, Joe from Winnipeg. Today I'm gonna be talkin' to you 'bout the NSF. Or maybe I should jus say NSF, if I say "the" NSF den you might tink I'm talkin' 'bout an organization der. An what's up with dat anyways eh? How come we got to make the names of stuff into letters. Like da NHL. Or da AMC. CFS. IBM. CBC. Does dat mean we're lazy? Or is it kine of like a nickname? I doan know. Maybe it's to make it soun more intimidatin' eh. I know if I'm dealin' with a place known by its letters it's either really big or else it can do scary tings. Like the CSIS eh? I doan even know what dat las one stans for it's so secret. So anyways, NSF. I got a bill back 'cause the cheque I wrote had the NSF eh. Not sufficient funs. I was waitin' for like a refun from the goverment. Well actually it was my frien's cheque, but I always like to be da one who has da good news an han dem der cheque like dey jus won da lottery eh. I tink dat would be a good job too. Hanin' out the lottery cheques to da winners. 'Cept I tink you'd get jealous after a while. Pretty soon you'd be, "How come dey get to be millionaires an not me?" Boy, dat's crazy. Anyways, instead of my frien's cheque. I get a bill. An the bill tells me my cheque was no good. Da NSF eh. So dey was informin' me dat dey wanted der money an dat dey were chargin' me for da bad cheque. An da bank was chargin' me for da bad cheque too eh. Boy, I jus felt like a criminal. Mad at myself. An mad at dese guys for chargin' me for my mistake. I didn't write dat cheque bad on purpose eh. Boy did I feel stupid eh. An embarass. An how come dey get to charge us for da mistake? What's up with dat? How come we doan get to charge dem money if dey make a mistake or fail to provide a service eh? We could jus walk in da bank der an say it's the kine of bank where der open but der's no teller service, an we could say, "Hey. You guys owe me 20 bucks. Plus I wan dis cheque cashed." Oh well, I guess it serves me right for not bein' more fiscally responsible eh. I should use our govern-ments as da example. Dey never write bad cheques. So after I tole my frien da bad news dat der cheque didn't arrive, she said, "Oh dat's OK. You know what happened to me?" "No," I says. An den she tells me the story of how a 'Nishnawbe on da street asked her for money 'cause he was NSF in his life eh. An she gave him some. An he said, "Tank you." An she said, "Meegwetch." An I guess dis guy never heard somebody who wasn't 'Nishnawbe talkin' his own language to him before eh. An she said his eyes lit up an she even taught he was gonna give her back da money he was so happy. Dat's a funny ting what can happen when we say what we mean in a way we unerstan eh? Maybe we call tings by letters like say, CFS or NSF, 'cause we're not too happy with what dey are eh? Sometimes I wish da places dat sent us money was more like our relatives. Instead of NSF dey could put a note in der, "Hey. Where's our money? An don't sen cheques. Cash or money order only." But den if dey was more like my famly I guess I'd take my time to pay dem back more. I keep gettin' surprised dat whenever I get in a bad mood 'cause of money or not havin' sufficien funs I get taught da same lesson over an over again. It's not dat importan eh. Money comes an goes, but stuff like the 'Nishnawbe guy on the street, you never forget dat. I can't remember none of all da money I've had. I'm Joe from Winnipeg. Meegwetch.

Moose on the Road

Hey you guys, this is me, Joe from Winnipeg. Today I'm gonna be talkin' to you 'bout moose on the road. I had dat dessert all prepared too, eh, an den I went an dropped it. "Oh no" I says out loud, "my mousse is on da road." Jus kiddin'. Das not da kine of mooses I mean. You know one ting I love about talkin' words out loud? You doan have to be too literate eh? Moose souns the same if it's da dessert or da animal or even da guy in da Archie comics. Moose. I tink da politicians like dat too, eh? 'Cause den if dey say someting like, say, "I need more time," an we say we waited long enough already, den dey could say, I'm talkin' bout the spices der. Or no could become k-no with a double o on der. Jus never stops eh. Even when day say "I doan lie," dey could mean dey sleep standin' up. It's a good ting promise means da same no matter how you say it. Anyways, boy I missed you guys. I fell asleep on the bus an ended up in Thompson eh. I woked up an I looked aroun an I said, "Where is dis beautiful place?" An den I saw some of dose Thompson turkeys eh. Big black birds. I'm not sure why dey're called

turkeys, maybe 'cause dat's da Tanksgivin' bird up der.
I doan know. So anyways, I figured I came dis far why
doan I go a little bit further. So I did. An den I ended up
in Gillam. More beauty up der, too. I even foun a shirt
der with my name on it. So I put dat on. An den I went
even further up north to Tadoule Lake. Wow. Das all I
could say eh. 'Cause it was beautiful an dey still have
der language an culture. I was jus jealous. An den I was
all ready to go on further adventures up in da north eh,
even past da North of 60, but I figured I should come
home. So I did. I ended up drivin' for my new frien
Conway. I got to drive an he got to sleep. What's up with
dat eh? How come da passengers always get to sleep,
not the driver? Anyways, I was tinkin': Man, dis place
we live in is BIG. Really big. An den I saw someone
walkin' on da road. Way far away. An I got all excited
'cause I was gonna pick dem up. Even if dey weren't
hitchhikin' I was gonna make dem a hitchhiker. An dat
road from Gillam is hilly eh. Imagine dat. Hills in Manitoba. I get so prairie-centric sometimes eh. Anyways, as
I get closer I see dat dis person on da road turns sideways an has four legs. In my head I was sayin, "Is dat
what I tink it is?" An my passenger said it out loud eh.
Dat kine of scared me for a minute 'cause dat's all he
said on da whole trip. An sure enough. Der it was. A
moose on da road. I wasn't even disappointed dat I
wouldn't have a hitchhiker now eh. I was jus happy to
see dat ole moose. So I drove all da way home. All four-
teen hours eh. Dat ole Conway jus kep sleepin'. I kep
havin' to stick my head out da window to stay awake

for a bit. You guys doan do dat eh. Drive sleepy. I'm not doin' dat never again. Anyways, I get home an I go for a hamburger. I hate to say it but dat moose made me hungry eh. I tink when some peoples who aren't 'Nishnawbe see a moose dey tink, "Ahhh Canada. I love dis country." Me. I look at mooses an tink, "Mmmm, supper." So anyways, I order dis burger an talk to my friens John an Roger an dis guy's starin' at me. An he says, "Are you Joe?" "Yeah" I says to him. An I was scared eh? 'Cause dis guy was big. An he had a beard. An I asked him how he knew my name an he said. "It's on yer shirt." "Oh," I says to him. An den he shakes my han an says, "I'm Thor." Boy I got scared again eh. Den I see dat Thor's like the moose. He's not what I'm tinkin' he is. An den we talk an he even says "Meegwetch" to me. An boy, dat warmed my heart. Someone who ain't 'Nishnawbe usin' dat language. So doan be like me an tink a person's a moose when really dey're somebody nice. I'm Joe from Winnipeg. Meegwetch.

Mix 'n No Match

Hey you guys, this is me, Joe from Winnipeg. Today I'm gonna be talkin' to you 'bout mix 'n no match. It's kine of strange for me, 'cause I don't even know what da mix 'n match is in the firs place eh? I'll get to dat in a secon. So to my new frien Nadine, who's out der goin' to school today, an to all of yous goin' to school, good for yous. Keep fillin' yer head with stuff dat'll help you some day. Even stuff you doan think you might use later, learn dat, too. You might fine yerself one day in a situation where evrybody's goin' what's the Pythagorus Theorum. Who knows dat? Quick. Lives is dependin' on it. I'm gettin' carried away der, but you never know. Maybe you guys might en up on a Canadian game show some day an win a real big prize, like a box of Kraft Dinner. So anyways, I was doin' all my laundry da other day eh. I was glad somebody else in da buildin' wasn't takin' my turn. Da only problem was, I was washin' all my clothes, so I had to wear dose clothes dat I never wear 'cause I didn't want to be wandrin' aroun in the basement naked eh. So I put on my white satin disco shirt with da big flares on da collar from about circus 1979. An I put on my polyester dress pants dat I wear if I go out. An for da shoes I had on rubber boots, 'cause I even had to wash my runners eh. Boy, I jus looked like a Wolseley area citizen eh. Jus kiddin'. Dose guys doan wear rubber boots. Anyways, I was hopin' I wouldn't get seen. An you notice whenever you hope you doan get seen by somebody you always en up gettin' seen. What's up with dat eh? I ran into my frien Darla. Right away she says to me, "Nice outfit der Joe. Way to mix 'n match." I said "Meegwetch" den I ran upstairs 'cause I was so embarrassed. I doan like people seein' me dressed up too good, 'cause den dey might tink dat I tink I'm all good eh. But I really wasn't all dat mixed 'n matched. I was more mixed 'n no match eh. 'Cause all my jeans was in da washer. I jus feel like da Einstein sometimes eh. I heard he only had one outfit. About seven times. All exactly da same. Me too. 'Cept I have jeans an a jean jacket instead of a professor shirt an a pipe. Anyways, all dis mix 'n no matchin' was makin' me wish I had some nice colour seprates der to wear eh. An even da 'lection for our new mayor. Der's gonna be some mix'n no matchin' goin' on der, too. We're gonna be mixin' up da city council. An der's gonna be no matchin' of opinions too eh. An when I say mixin' up da city council I mean changin' it. Not confusin' dem. Let dem confuse demselves. An sometimes when we mix stuff up dat ain't s'posed to go together we get good tings eh. Look at da peanut butter an chocolate. An da Regis an Kathie Lee. Boy, even bannock 'n lard. Lard's not jus for cookin' with, you can eat it, too. So I hope you guys get out der an vote. An tink about who yer votin' for, too. Doan jus show up der an look at da names an be all mixed up an pick the ones dat match yer eenie meenie miney mo. Make da informed choices eh. I'm Joe from Winnipeg. Meegwetch.

Immunizin'

Hey you guys, this is me, Joe from Winnipeg. Today I'm gonna be talkin' to you 'bout immunizin'. *(Shudder.)* I hate needles eh. Well I guess we got a new mayor eh? Good luck to dem. An good luck to us. Da people have spoken. Les hope we're sayin' a good ting. So. Da other day I was cuttin' through the bank so dat I wouldn't haf to go 'round the corner outside eh. I sometimes feel guilty when I cut corners like dat, but den dat's as close as I'll get to bein' a finance minister. An dat makes me tink too, eh. If you take a square of something, say, a piece of paper an you cut off all da corners, don't you still got a square? What's up with dat? Anyways, I see my frien Kelly in der eh. He was doin' what you always do in a bank, if yer not takin' a shortcut through it. Stan in line eh. So I see him an we say hello an talk an shake hans an do all dat frienly stuff. An den I says to him, "Hey Kelly, why doan you go move dose little tings dat are steerin' you guys to da tellers. Make a little pattern or someting. Or else even turn aroun in line an preten you're at da front." He gave me a horror look on his face eh. I guess when it comes to us Canadians you doan mess aroun with da standin' in line. "I'm jus kidding," I tole him, an I touched his arm. Boy did he ever scream. Den I got scared 'cause I taught, man, dis guy's takin' dis way too serious, but he calmed me down. "Dat's OK Joe. My arm's sore 'cause I got immunized." "Immunize? Like when you get dat little ting dat leaves a funny little mark on yer arm? Some people looks like a little flower. Some people looks like dey leaned on a cigrette. An some people—" "Yeah. Yeah Joe," he says to me. "Dat's it." "Where do you go to get dis immunizin'?" I asked him. An he says da doctor, but he didn't recommend me doin' it if I already got all my shots. He says he jus does dat 'cause he likes protecin' himself. An he has a mile case of hypochondria dat he wishes he could get immunize for. So I lef an continued my cuttin' through da bank. An I was tinkin' 'bout dat immunize a lot eh. At firs I was kine of scared. What if I go an get da lock jaws 'cause I doan have my shot? I'd be talkin' like da Kirk Douglas. Doan you get dat from steppin' on a nail or someting sharp like dat? Isn't a needle sharp? How come we doan get it from da needle? What's up with dat? Boy, my little head was jus spinnin'. I even had to shake it like in da cartoon. All dis immunizin'. An all da ways we try protec ourselves from not gettin' hurt eh. Some of us lockin' ourselves in our houses. Some of us tryin' not to tink about stuff. An some of us even shuttin' ourselves off from other human bein's so's we won't get hurt. But you know what? Der's no guarantees eh. You can do all dis an still get hurt. I'm not sayin' doan protec yourself, jus doan let it get in da way of livin' yer lives eh. I'm Joe from Winnipeg. Meegwetch.

La la la

Hey you guys, this is me, Joe from Winnipeg. Today I'm gonna be talkin' to you 'bout someting very strange. Dat ting when you go "la la la" an cover yer ears wit yer hans and close yer eyes. Whatever dat ting is, dat's what I'm gonna talk about. So how 'bout all dat election inquiry eh? What's up with dat? I know der's rules an procedures but I sometimes wish dey would let peoples like us go der an be da inquiry. Den we could be like a parent eh. "Did you do dis?" "Yes?" "How come?" "I doan know." "OK, dat's it yer grounded." I'm jus kiddin' der. I know dis is serious. I tink dat grounding can be pretty effective punishment. So anyways, da other day I ran into my frien Ron. He's a machiness up der in Flin Flon. What is a flin anyways? Or a flon for dat matter. Anyhow, Ron was walkin' aroun coverin' up his ears, closin' his eyes an goin' "la la la". Boy I had to go stop him before he walked into a pole eh. "Ron. Ron." I says to him. "What're you doin'?" "Oh. Joe," he says to me. "I was jus makin' da world go away." "How come?" I ask him. An he tells me 'bout how some guy was talkin' to him 'bout da election inquiry, an Quebec an maybe another referendum, an da election results in da 'nunited

States an... Boy, by dis time I was coverin' my ears goin' "la la la I can't hear you". Boy, dat works pretty good. An you doan even have to say "la la la." You can say "no no no," or whatever you want eh. So I tried to say "bye" to Ron, but he couldn't hear me. He jus wen walkin' into poles an stuff, but at lease he seemed happy. An I was happy too. So I wen home an turned on da TV. An der was a story on der 'bout da floods in Central America. An I changed da channel real fas eh. Boy, den I realize dat was da same ting as coverin' my ears an goin' "la la la". So even dough I didn't want to, I changed da channel back an watched dat story. 'Bout people losin' everytin' eh. All da hardship an sorrow. Boy...I couldn't figure out why I was watchin' dis eh. Der's already so much bad stuff in da world. An da news jus seems to give us more of it. But den I realize eh. Dat's part of my responsibility. We always talk 'bout how lucky we are dat we live in dis wonerful country. An it is a great gift, but it also means we have to help dose ones who ain't so lucky eh. We shouldn't be coverin' our ears an closin' our eyes to peoples who needs our help. Me, I'm gonna fine a way to help dose peoples, even if it means jus prayin' for dem. You know, even if you don't got material tings you can always help out in other ways too eh. I tink dat's when we truly see ourselves as human bein's, when we give to one anothers eh. Thas why Christmas is so great eh. An birthday parties. Anniversaries. Pretty much any place where dey got presents. I hope you guys see an hear lots today. I'm Joe from Winnipeg. Meegwetch.

Peekaboo

Hey you guys, this is me, Joe from Winnipeg. Today I'm gonna be talkin' to you 'bout peekaboo. Is dat one word or not? Boy, I doan know. Maybe if you have to spell dat word today you better put some hyphen in der jus to be safe. Otherwise you might en up with peoples correctin' yer spellin' for you. Das a funny ting about dat eh. I'm not sure how to react. Like are you s'posed to say tank you when someone tells you you spelt say da word "ere" wrong. Like it's sposed to be E R R, not E R E. Maybe you could say, "To err is human." Even dough I tink dat should be said da way it souns eh, "errrr". Among da 'Nishnawbe whenever you make dat soun, "errr", it means like, "ever sick", or "dat's crazy". Anyways, 'nough 'bout spellin'. Back to da peekaboos. So I was playin' dat game eh. Peekaboo. Wit one of my little nephews. I love dat game 'cause it doan cos nothin' eh. An you can use whatever you got handy. Like a newspaper. Or da corner of da couch. Or even yer hans. So der we was, me an my nephew. Playin' peekaboo. An I would be jumpin' aroun tryin' to hide from him eh. An den I'd jump out an say "surprise". Den my nephew says to me, "Uncle. Yer s'posed to say peekaboo. Not "surprise". An what does dat mean anyways, peek a boo? What's up with dat?" Boy, I was jus jarred eh. I didn't even know what to say. So den I did dat ting dat adults an da governments do all the time eh. I tried an make what I just said make sense. "Oh, uhh, I said 'surprise' because I knew you wouldn't like me to say peekaboo." But really I jus forgot to say peekaboo, I was jus too embarrass to admit I screwed up eh. Den my nephew says, "Les not play dis anymore. Let's do da crossword puzzle instead." Boy, dey grow up so fas eh. Here he is wantin' to do da crossword an he's only in Grade 8. Oh well. But den sometin' else happened eh. I got a call dat my brother was in da hospital. So I rush right over der eh. An after I see dat my brother's gonna be OK we had to get him dressed eh. He was sore an evrything, so he needed help. Boy, all you guys, who help people get dressed, dat's a good ting yer doin'. Dey appreciate it eh. An I appreciate it now, too. It's not easy. Anyways, I was helpin' him pull his shirt over his head der eh. An when his head popped out I jus went, peekaboo. Boy, dat was dangerous eh. If he hadn't been so sore he might've hit me eh. Da look on his face. "Doan make me laugh," he says to me. "It hurts." Boy, dat's a funny ting eh. Dat laughin' can hurt. Strange dat. But den dat's what dis peekaboo makes me tink too, eh. Our lives is so fragile eh. An our bodies. We should have little stamps on us der dat say dat, "Fragile". Sos we can remember to take care of ourselves eh. 'Cause boy, one minute you could be playin' peekaboo wit yer nephew an da next yer helpin' somebody put on der underwears. I guess we gotta 'member life does a peekaboo on us all da time eh. Sometimes good. Sometimes bad. We jus gotta make sure we keep on keepin' on. An if you need help, ask somebody eh. Der's all dese good people out der who help other people witout even askin' evry day. An if one of yous figures out what dat peekaboo means, let me an my nephew know eh. We wanna make a crossword puzzle for dat. 'Cep I doan know what da clue might be. Eight letter word dat's not surprise. This is Joe from Winnipeg. Meegwetch.

Mats

Hey you guys, this is me, Joe from Winnipeg. Today I'm gonna be talkin' to you 'bout mats. But first. Did you guys watch the debate of the century der las night? Da one dat was gonna decide the future of Quebec? An Canada? Man oh man. I went an missed it eh. But it's a good ting for that CPAC channel, else I never would've seen it. That crazy channel's on like number 70 or someting like dat. I jus about twisted my arm off der, turnin' da channel changer knob aroun. I didn't know how to use dat converter ting right, eh. Boy, I saw da Quebec leaders arguin' der. What's up with dis? I was sayin' out loud to da TV. Dat's how you can tell when someone's really mad eh. Dey're talkin' to da TV. Anyways, What's up with dis? I says to the TV. I can't even unerstan what dey're sayin' dey're all talkin' over each other. Maybe dese guys should arm wrestle or something instead eh. Dey could even put dat on da pay per view. At lease den dis debate wouldn't be like da las five or so dat I've seen. Da ole commentators would be goin', "Well, what'd you tink of dat debate?" "No clear winner. Again." "Where's dat John Turner when you need him eh?" So. Mats. Rugs. Whatever. Dose tings you lay on da floor. I seem to be tinkin' 'bout stuff dat gets walked on a lot lately eh. Like even me myself. I get walked on all da time. Literal an figural eh. I had my back walked on by my cousin after I seen Mr. Bentley gettin' dat done on da Jefferson's. Boy, dat wasn't a good idea eh. He tole me he felt his foot touch da floor when he did dat. He mus've missed my spine. Makes sense dough. Gettin' walked on an bein' spineless goes han in han. So I saw my frien Sig da other day eh. An he was layin' out a mat on da floor of dis business, 'cause dat's what Sig does. He works in mats. An I figured I'd impress him der eh. So I says, "'S'cuse me, Sig. Is dat mat a rib needle variety? Wit da anti-bacterial backin'? Charcoal covered? An da produc must be laid flat. Do not stan on ens?" An he says to me, "Joe, what you talkin' bout? It's a mat." "Oh," I said. I guess he knew I was tryin' to show off. I remembered dat stuff from when I used to clean floors eh. I was always forgetin' to lay dem flat like da instructions said. An I stood dem on der ens too, eh. Dat mus've been why Sig let me go. Anyways, I said to Sig, "Sig. What's da secret to layin' out mats?" An he says to me, "Joe, da thing about mats is, you wanna make sure you can see what's under dem. 'Cause you'd be surprised." Den I let Sig do his work, 'cause he takes pride in his job eh. Boy, dat's true eh. You wanna make sure what's under 'em. Dat's da same too with mattresses an couch cushions eh. I bet some of yous are hidin' dat stain you or your pet made by flippin' dem over. So den when company, your parents or your snoopy in-laws come over you can preten like everytin's A-OK. Dat's alright to do dat too, flippin' the cushions or da mattress. I do it at my friens' places all da time after I visit, an dey never know. So all dis talk about mats an makin' sure we can see what's under 'em, dat's a good lesson for us. For our government. Where we work. Our famlies too eh. We gotta make sure we can see what's goin' on. 'Cause I'm gettin' dis funny feelin' stuff's bein' swept under da mat too much lately. If it's yer house an company's comin' dat's OK, but not our institutions. Dey're da mats, an we're the snoopy in-laws eh. An to dose of you out der who ain't feelin' too good, I pray you get better. This is Joe from Winnipeg. Meegwetch.

Great Expectations

Hey you guys, this is me, Joe from Winnipeg. Today I'm gonna be talkin' to you 'bout *Great Expectations*. Les examine dat work a little bit. Now I tink dat in dat novel, Dickens, bein' the master storyteller dat he was, was intrested in examinin' da human condition. You guys knew I was kiddin' right. Dat's not da kine of great expectations I mean. But der is a tip der for you who have to explain or give yer 'pinion 'bout somethin'. Jus say it's got to do with da human condition. When I went to school I used to put dat for my answer all da time. Da teacher der would ask me, "Joe, what did Shakespeare mean when he wrote da *Hamlet*." "Human condition," I'd say. An den my teacher would jus smile an say, "Dat is correc." Boy dat's a good catch-all answer so's dat you look smart eh. But be careful to change da subjec right away or else you might get caught. Like say someone says, "So, what do you think about da economic situation right now?" An den you say, "Oh. It's da human condition all over again eh." An den dey'll nod an agree wit you. Den you say sometin' like, "Hey, what's up with dis weather eh?" An hey. What is up wit dis weather? Das really what I'm talkin' 'bout today eh. Da great expectation. As in da winter. Where is it? I got to tell you guys I'm gettin' freaked out. Las night I was throwin' out da garbage an I jus about got runned over by four peoples on bikes. Bikes yet. What's up with that? It's the en of November already an dese guys are ridin' bikes. An why not eh? I guess dat's alright. It jus all seems kine of unnatural to me dough. Kine of like dat new haircut Preston Manning got eh. I know dat's ole news, but I can't get dat ole picture of him out of my head. I guess I kine of expected him to look da same all da time eh. Like my dad. He's had da same haircut for about fifty years. So I'm kine of use to his head lookin' a certain way. But I got to tell you one other strange ting eh. I was goin' to da store da other day. An boy are der ever lots of shoppers out der. Anyways, I go to dat store an when I was goin' in, da door didn't open eh. So I just stood der for a little bit. An den I realized what I was doin'. "Joe." I says to myself, "What are you doin'? Are you expectin' dat door to open by itself for you or something?" Boy, you know what? I was eh. I'm so used to da automatic doors now dat I was expectin' dat one to jus open up for me without me doin' anything. An dat's kine of a scary ting eh. I guess all expectations are. Whether dey're great or small. We may be expectin' dem to turn out good, or we may be expectin' dem to turn out bad, but it's dat waitin' an expectin' dat's scary. So. I guess what I'm sayin' is, whatever great expectation you have for today I hope you fine it. An you know what, I was tinkin' no matter how bad we expect a day to turn out dey'res always sometin' good in der eh. Even if it's jus goin' home. Or even goin' to bed. I hope yer great expectation is realized today. An remember dat da winter is comin' eh. This is Joe from Winnipeg. Meegwetch.

Leavin' the Lights On

Hey you guys, this is me, Joe from Winnipeg. Today I'm gonna be talkin' to you 'bout leavin' the lights on. Boy, what's up with dis Bill Clinton ting eh? Impeach da guy. Censure him. I doan know 'bout all dat stuff, but what's up with not listenin' to the people der in America eh. Dey jus want to get back to worryin' 'bout da Christmas shoppin' and freakin' out over havin' da famly over for dinner. Who's gonna sit where an who's gonna carve the turkey. But den I guess I shouldn't be too surprised. We elect dose people on trust. Once dey're in office it's hard to get rid of dem. I guess dat's what da impeach is all about eh. Dat's 'merican business anyways. When dey start talkin' 'bout da impeachment of da Chrétien, dat's when we got to really pay attention. Hard to say what would have to happen to cause dat eh. Maybe him jus doin' whatever he wants. Not keepin' promises. Not listenin' to us. Wait a minute. Ahh, dat's too much politics already. Der's better tings to hear first ting in da mornin' eh. Like da kettle whistlin'. Or da fridge door openin'. Maybe even da soun of da garbage truck eh.

So. Leavin' da lights on. It's been kine of strange for me lately eh. I was visitin' one of my frien's, Rick. He's a bus driver eh. My other frien Rick makes cabinets. So. Rick da bus driver an I went to go for coffee. An we were gettin' ready to go out der, puttin' on our coats an we're goin' out da door. An I says, "Hey Rick. You're leavin' da lights on." An he says, "I know. Dat's so da robbers will tink I'm home." "What robbers?" I tell him. An he says, "Whoever might want to break in my home." So we go to coffee. But all night I'm tinkin' 'bout dat eh. Leavin' da lights on so you tink someone's home. If I leave my lights on I get mad. 'Cause den I got to pay more for da hydro. I doan worry 'bout someone breakin' in 'cause der's nothin' to take. Unless somebody wants ole boxes an a couch with dirty arm rests. Den I tink of all da other reasons to leave da lights on. Maybe 'cause yer scared of da dark. Maybe 'cause you jus want to see where you're goin'. Lights can be useful dat way. Or else maybe you want to leave da lights on for somebody else eh. To let dem know you really are home. So when you come back home after a long day workin', der's da lights on. Maybe dat's why I been feelin' a little strange eh. I been lonesome for other people. Not for me. 'Cause I'm very lucky with my many friens. But I know some of yous is missin' people you love dis Christmas eh. Maybe you can write dem a letter. Or else send dem a lightbulb to remine dem dat you've got a light in yer heart for dem. Den too, dey might get da lightbulb an tink, what's up with this? Busted up pieces of glass an some filament for Christmas. Tanks a lot. Boy, maybe even poor old Bill Clinton. Dat's what dey'll say to him. "Don't leave da lights on in da White House der Bill. Jus leave da keys under da mat." An to all you guys who leave yer Christmas lights on. Meegwetch. You help make our hearts light. An doan worry 'bout takin' dem down. If you forget about dem for say, six months den you can jus go, Oh well, Christmas is almos here again. I'll jus leave the lights on the house. This is Joe from Winnipeg. Meegwetch.

Christmas

Hey you guys, this is me, Joe from Winnipeg. Today I'm gonna be talkin' to you 'bout Christmas. I just found out a strange ting the other day. I celebrate my favrit holiday tonight. Like da French people. At midnight eh. Dat's when Joe an his famly opens der presents. We tried to open presents on Christmas morning like I foun out most people do, 'cept we all slept in eh. So we figured we'd go back to da way it was. I foun dis out from my frien Tom eh. We were talkin' 'bout da holidays an dis opening da presents on Christmas eve ting came out eh. We was both shocked with each other eh. I heard da rumours 'bout openin' yer presents on da Christmas day, but I never seen it eh. An he heard rumours of da midnight Christmas Eve celebrations too, but he never seen it eh. It's good when you fine out about a new tradition. I just assumed most people did the midnight thing too, eh. Instead of jus some of us 'Nishnawbe an da French. I guess we can see da birth of the Métis people in dat common Christmas celebration. Although I guess da 'Nishnawbe didn't have Christmas like we do now. But da idea of love an respect we get with dis season was usehly around eh. Boy, listen to me, just babbling on eh. Get to da point Joe. I will. I will. But first. What's up with dis Christmas eh? It feels like a good one. Is dat just me? Or is it evrybody? I hope so. 'Cause I want you guys to feel good tings as da 1998 ends eh. Tink of da year as a real big meal. An we're jus gettin' to the dessert part right now. Whatever you favrit dessert might be. Pumpkin pie maybe. Or else choclate ice cream. Maybe even da Christmas pudding eh. So. da point. Oh yeah. Christmas. It's been hard for me to focus lately eh. If you were tryin' to fix something on yer car an I was the guy holdin' the flashlight you'd be pretty mad at me right now eh. I'd prob'ly be hummin', lookin' aroun. Wondrin' if der's dose little fuzzy tings in my belly button eh. Tinkin' how I'll save removin' dose for later eh. I feel sorry for you guys with da outies eh? You don't get to do dat, but den maybe yer more hygenic or someting. I've been unfocused for a simple reason eh. I feel good. I know dere's always bad stuff goin' on in da world. An I'm not sayin' to ignore it all da time. But you got to take a break sometimes too, eh. Jus fine one minute. One measly little minute in da day to reflect. Think of something funny. Or happy. Or stupid. If you have trouble with dat last one, jus tink of me eh. Dat should help. I suggest dis, 'cause doin' dis is what made me feel good. I was runnin' aroun tryin' to do all da tings I forgot dis Christmas. Presents. Cards. Whatever. An I even missed my bus. So. I had to take a forced time out eh. All dis happened when it was snowing der da other night. An I was waitin' in da bus shelter for da next bus, wishin' I could sit down without gettin' a cold bum. What's up with those metal seats eh? Cold in the winter. Hot in the summer. Anyways, I started starin' ahead eh. At nothin' in paticular. An I see dis couple eh. Draggin' home a Christmas tree. 'Cept I tink dey was arguin' about which way to drag it eh. Top first. Or bottom first. It looked like a male female kine of argument. But den dey hugged an dragged da tree sideways eh. Boy. Dat made me tink. Right der is something more powerful dan love eh. Forgiveness. An dat's what Christmas is to me. Forgivin'. Forgivin' life if it's been rough to you. Forgivin' yer loved ones. Even yer hated ones too, eh. To shop is human eh. To forgive. Dat's Christmas. Merry Christmas my friends. This is Joe from Winnipeg. Meegwetch.

New Year's

Hey you guys, this is me, Joe from Winnipeg. Today I'm gonna be talkin' to you 'bout New Year's. Boy it's da 1999 eh. Dat makes me tink 'bout lots of tings. Da song by dat guy who's name I can't remember. Boy, dat's a good way to make sure you're forgotten eh. Jus get rid of yer name. Say da tax people was lookin' for you, it could be like, "Did you see…?" "Who?" "Dat guy." "Which guy?" "You know. Da one." "No. What's der name?" "I forget." But dat's not good. 'Cause we're not peoples if we don't remember eh. Boy, I'm even tinkin' of dat TV show, *Space 1999*. Da one with Martin Landau. Der on da moon. An da moon gets sent out of orbit or someting. 'Member dat show? Boy, if you doan, maybe dat's a good ting. The more TV we forget prob'ly da more like peoples we are eh. So. New Year's. I was gonna make a list for you guys eh. Da best dis. An da best dat. Of da past year. But I tink sometimes lists get made jus to cause trouble eh. Like say I do a list of da best foods of 1998. I could say, number one: potatoes. Any kind. Number two: turnips. Number tree: char-grilled moose meat, seasoned, served au jus, sautéed onions, field mushrooms along with a ginger an tomato compote an a side of Kraft Dinner an ketchup. An right away, somebody's gonna say, "Joe. You never serve ketchup with moose meat. Mustard maybe. But for sure no ketchup." An den too, somebody might say, "You got too many root vegetables in yer list" eh. An who cares anyways. Da best parts of da past year are whatever you choose. I always used to get confused at da New Year's eh. I couldn't tell if it was represent by da baby with a beard or da old guy with diapers or whatever. An dat's da funny ting 'bout New Year's eh. Dis artificial line. Jus like a map. It says we're in Manitoba right now. An you see lines drawn all over da place on maps. Dis border an dat border. All artificial eh. I tink dat's why da 'Nishnawbe was so confused when peoples first came here. Puttin' little sticks in da groun an sayin' dis is mine. Dat's yours. I tink maybe da Earth is nobody's. And everybody's. So anyways, we're all tole dat dis is da end of da century. Da end of da millennium. Some say it's really da year 2000 dat's da last one, but I tink when dat one is gonna become a two, 1999 is da end year eh. It's all gonna be big eh. History. Some people say da dawn of a new, better age for peoples. Others say it's da end of time. I doan know 'bout all dat stuff. But I foun a new way of lookin' at da New Year's eh. It kine of is like a line. But not one dat's straight. It's one dat's a circle eh. Dis lovely winter dat we're all freezin' in right now is da winter of 1998. But it's also da winter of 1999. It continues eh. So when dis year ends an da next one begins, to me, it's not a total new beginnin'. It's more like sittin' on top of dat circle. Gettin' ready to go round again eh. An when da 2000 year comes, it'll be da same ting for all of us. We'll get up. An make breakfast. An da same shows'll be on da radio. An yer job will hopefully still be der. But der will be one diffrence eh. Prob'ly nobody will forget da new year when dey're makin' out cheques. So I hope you guys have a Happy New Year's with lots of kisses. An hope. An continuation. This is Joe from Winnipeg. Meegwetch.

3D's

Hey you guys, this is me, Joe from Winnipeg. Today I'm gonna be talkin' to you 'bout 3D's. Did you guys see the hockey game on da TV last night. Boy dat was great. Even dough we lost. It was still good seein' da hockey night in Winnipeg again. No disrespec to da Moose. But I did always wonder why dey named demselves after big slow animals dat are good to eat. What's up with that eh? If you name a sports team after an animal it should instill da fear in da opponent eh. Like say da Mighty Ducks. If dey was just called da Ducks people would laugh at dem. But you put might in der an boy you're talkin' scary. Maybe we could have da Mighty Moose. Maybe not. All I know is, I keep hearin' people sayin', "What's wrong with da professional sports? What's wrong with da hockey?". Look at what was goin' on here in Manitoba eh. Looks kine of right to me. So anyways, 3D's. Well I kine of mislead you der. Sorry. Since da 3D is s'posed to be so excitin' I thought I'd use dat. I've been hearin' how they got da 3D pictures. An 3D sound. So that these 'lectronic experiences are more real. What's wrong with real? Reality's a nice place to 'scape from eh, but I still wanna live der. So the 3D I'm talkin' 'bout is really jus one "D". Three times. It's decisions eh. Decisions. Decisions. Decisions. I was talkin' with my frien da other day. She had so many decisions she had to make in her life dat one day. With one big decision piled on da top. Boy, she was just askin' me for help eh. "Joe. What should I do?" she said. "I doan know," I tole her. Sometimes coffee's good black. Sometimes good with sugar. Sometimes milk. Sometimes both. I doan know." "Thanks," she says to me. "Yer lots of help." An I said, "Meegwetch." But den I kine of got in a little bit trouble for not reconizin' her sarcastic tone eh. Oh well. But it makes me tink about all da decisions we make every day. What to wear. Do I put on new underwears today. Do I sleep a little bit more an catch da later bus. Do I turn left. Do I turn right. Do I buy dis. Do I eat dat. Boy der's too many. It's a woner some of us decide anythin' at all eh. An dat's a decision too. Doin' nothin'. An it's easy to forget too eh, dat everythin' we decide has an effec. It's like dat game with da marbles an da plastic sticks. Ker plunk I tink dey call it. You pull out dat stick an it's OK. An maybe you pull dat stick an all da marbles fall. But it's da power of dat decision eh. So whatever you guys decide today. Whether it's big or small. Jus remember dat it's one of our greatest gifts as human bein's eh. Da power to decide. You always got choice. Even if yer say decidin' between eatin' da black jelly bean, which you may hate, an da pink jelly bean, which you may hate more. Der's still choice der eh. Sometimes we worry 'bout what's da right decision an we go "hmmm" an "I doan know…" An we forget to 'member how powerful choices make us eh. Da decisions are like da underwears eh. We got da power to change dem. Me, I usehly go with my firs instinc. 'Cause even if da firs "D's" not so good I still got two "D's" left eh. I'm Joe from Winnipeg. Meegwetch.

Coffee cups and Donuts

Hey you guys, this is me, Joe from Winnipeg. Today I'm gonna be talkin' to you 'bout coffee cups and donuts. I couldn't really decide which of dose to talk about so I picked both, but then I foun out they're kine of the same thing. Speakin' of the coffee cups, did you guys see that new commercial on da TV with the Terry MacLeod. Walkin' dere with a coffee cup an some kine of attached case. When I first saw dat I thought, "Man, dat guy's crazy walkin' aroun with dat coffee cup at night. Don't he know someone might try take dat from him?" But den I thought, "Hey Joe. You shouldn't live in fear man. Dat's not cool." An then I thought, "How come Terry MacLeod's walkin' aroun da streets at night with a coffee cup?" What's up with that? Maybe he lost it a little bit or something. He seemed fine though da las time I sawn him. I was comin' in to talk to you guys on the radio and he was gettin' out of dis big white limousine wit da sunglasses on. Come to tink of it, dat was at night too, eh? Maybe he's doin' this strange behaviour 'cause he's da "maverick" eh. Him an James Garner. So anyways, coffee cups an donuts. I was given a coffee cup for Christmas eh. An boy, dat's a good gift. It can last for years an years. Till da paint comes off it even. I mus have coffee cups in my house from da forties eh. An it doesn't matter who you give da coffee cup to, it'll always work as a present eh. You can wrap it up there. Hand it to dem. "Here you go my frien. It's for you." "Oh what is it?" "It's a coffee cup filled with stuff." You know how they put jelly beans or candy in there. Sometimes even coffee. Anyways, I took my cup to the coffee shop to get some milk. I didn't want to stain my bran new cup jus yet. An when I was der I ordered a donut too eh. So I sit down. An den dis strange guy walks in off da street eh. An I think, "Is dat Terry MacLeod? Oh no. It's just my frien Angus." So we talk a bit. An he asks me what I'm doin'. Even dough he can see I'm drinkin' milk in a coffee cup an eatin' a donut. An he says to me, "Joe. Did you know dat dat coffee cup an dat donut are the same ting?" "What do you mean?" I says. 'Cause now I tink this guy really is crazy eh. An he tells me "Dey're both one-sided objects." An I go, "Hunh." "Yeah sure." he says. An he explains to me, an you got to tink about this. Stay with me here. Picture da handle of da coffee cup. An now picture da hole donut. They're kine of the same shape. Now imagine dat da cup part of coffee cup puffs up like a balloon. 'Ventually you'd get a funny lookin' donut shape, but it would be like a donut. Dis took me about seven hours to figure out. But it is true. Dey're both one-sided objects eh. I never thought dat something one-sided could be useful or so tasty. Course one-sided wins are good, too. But not when we want da truth eh. Dat's where one side's not enough. Dat's why I'm glad we're findin' out about da vote splitting. An da trial in da States der. Fairness is good. 'Cause boy I remember when I was a kid an I'd get in a fight with my brother. An my dad would say, "OK Joe. Let's hear your side of it." "Well—" "Go to your room." I hope you guys express your 'pinions today. Tell your side eh. An if you want something, make sure you ask for it. I'm Joe from Winnipeg. Meegwetch.

Rubber Boots

Hey you guys, this is me, Joe from Winnipeg. Today I'm gonna be talkin' to you 'bout rubber boots. But firs, I gotta say someting again. I'm walkin' 'round da city da other day. Lookin' at stuff. Window shoppin'. Although I doan know why it's called dat. You doan actually shop for windows dat way, although dat would be a good way to know if it's da kine you like. An we can't buy what's behind da window, so...what's up with that? But anyways, I'm tinkin' 'bout tings that are goin' on in da world eh. An I can't figure out how everyting got so imbalance. People killin' one anothers. People discussin' how many refugees to let in da country. Come on you guys. Most of yous is refugees or descendants of dem. Whether by choice or by force. I wish dese guys would learn dat you can't get possessive over a land you don't own. Nobody owns it. Right? An speakin' of dat, what's up with da premier? "I doan unerstand what dese people want." I can't believe I was gonna vote for dis guy. Maybe 'Nishnawbe will create alternative Conservative party to split vote. Somethin like Reform party, 'cept less understandin'. Den if dey run in election da leader can say, "I doan unerstand what you voters want. So you should vote for me. 'Cause if I'm dis out of touch, 'magine how—." OK I'm jus kiddin' der. Sorry 'bout dat. So. Rubber boots. OK. I figure I go buy new rubber boots, 'cause my ole ones had a little tiny hole in der eh. An da water collects in der an yer foot makes dat "squish squish" soun eh. I wore a plastic bag on my foot 'couple times but den I figured what's da point of havin' rubber boots if you need to wear waterproof lining for dem to work. So I went an bought new ones. Good ting 'bout rubber boots. Dey're still pretty cheap. So I'm lookin' at dem in da store, wondrin' if I'll get da black ones with da red tip. Or black ones with da green tip. Hmmm. Den I run into my frien who don't want me to name him. But he lives in big house an used to drive a bright orange Volkswagen Beetle eh. An he's English. An he's goin' to someplace call Dubai. At first when he tole me he was goin' Dubai. I said "dubai what?" "No. Dubai." "I know. Dubai what?" "Not what. Dat's da place." "What's da place?" "No. What's on second." Den he laughs. Boy, it took me 'bout fifteen minutes to fine out Dubai is a city in da Middle East. What you goin' der for I ask my unnamed English frien with a big house an used to have bright orange Beetle. Oh I'm goin' window shoppin'. Yeah right. He's buyin' some cool clothes 'cause it's hot in dis Dubai place. Gotta stay comfortable, he tells me. So I wish him a good trip an I buy black rubber boots with green tips. Would have preferred da traditional rubber boots, but dey didn't have my size. So I can't wait to get home and put on my new rubber boots. An I go for a walk. An I walk through all kines of puddles eh. Der's something very liberatin' about dat. Walkin' through puddles. I highly recommend dat to you guys. An as I'm walkin' I tink. Hmmm. Dat's funny. I'm really only wearin' rubber boots for one reason eh. Comfort. An I think of all da tings in our lives dat we have for comfort. In fact, seems like most of what we do is for da comfort eh. Whether dat's work to buy a nice chair, or however it is you take it easy. I guess you could even argue dat everythin in our lives an what motivates us has to do with tryin' to make ourselves comfortable, from my frien an his cool clothes to me an my rubber boots. We sure don't like cold, wet feets eh? Maybe today when you realize one of da many tings dat makes you comfortable you can say little prayer for all dose people who aren't so comfortable. I'm Joe from Winnipeg. Meegwetch.

Piggybacks

Hey you guys, this is me, Joe from Winnipeg. Today I'm gonna be talkin' to you 'bout piggybacks. How you guys doin' today? Are you ready for everythin' dat life's gonna throw at you? We never seem to be eh, yet we manage somehow. What's up with that? So. Piggybacks. I was wondrin' 'bout dat word piggybacks. We all know what it means, but why is it called dat eh? Why not horseybacks? We sure ride dose more dan we do pigs. 'Cept my dad an his brother. When dey were boys on da farm dey had to look after dese two piglets. An dey did, but den dey started playin' with dem. Doin' wheelbarrow races with dem. An even gettin' for-real piggybacks. Boy, came time to…well, you know what happens to pigs on da farm, an my dad an his brother couldn't eat dat dinner eh. But evrybody was amaze at how lean dat meat was. So anyways, I seen dis young woman giving piggyback ride to a little boy eh. An was dat ever sweet. I forgot all about piggybacks. Dat's funny how we can forget about someting until we see it again. Like say, ole frens. Or pack of Freshie with da little bird on it. Even ole style box of Beep with little happy bird saying "beep" on der. Maybe dey'll bring dat back as baby boomer nostalgia. Classic Beep dey can call it. Anyways, I was 'membering how we used to play chicken fights. Where you piggyback somebody an you try knock each other down. 'Member dat game? Why it's called chicken fight I doan know. More like da bumping into each other till somebody falls over fight. An it's sad how much dat word "fight" is in tings we do. Maybe dat's why der's still so much stupid war goin' on amoung us human bein's. But I gotta say, I had fun playin' games like dat. Or givin' piggyback rides to people. Now yer wondrin', What's da point of da piggyback ting Joe. Well. Lots been goin' on eh? Like I said. Life always throwin' stuff at us. Tings I doan understan eh? Like da big one. Dis war dat's goin' on. They're still not callin' it dat yet. It's only "conflict" for now. Or da nurse strike in Saskatchewan. NDP government legislatin' workers back to work? I'm not arguin' ethics over dat, but dat would kine of be like Conservative government spendin' lots of money on healthcare and raising tax on business eh. Know what I mean? An den here I'm readin' paper an I see dat relative of mine dies in jail. Again. Not blamin' anybody. But why do tings like dis keep happenin' to people? What's up with all of it? An den I tink. Boy. It'd be great if der was somebody to piggyback me through all dese questions eh. All da rough spots in life. Don't have to worry 'bout question or answer. Just get piggyback through it. Life says, here's bad news Joe. No problem. I got piggyback. Den I tink. Hey I do got piggyback in a way. Whether dat's friens. Family. Stranger. Prayer. Der's lots of way to get piggyback through rough spots eh. So I hope you guys fine dose piggybacks to help you with what life throw at you eh. Whatever it is. If it's person you see who's stronger dan you. Just jump on der back. Well not literal. You might hurt dem. Someone did dat to me an we both ended up like pancake on da groun. Mmmm. Pancake. An sausage. OK. Now I'm hungry. I'm Joe from Winnipeg. Meegwetch.

Loonie Game

Hey you guys, this is me, Joe from Winnipeg. Today I'm gonna be talkin' to you 'bout da loonie game. I'll 'splain what dat is in a minute. You know, I love commentating to you guys, but sometimes der's tings dat happen an I wanna commentate on but I don't know what useful stuff I'm addin' to what already been said eh. Like dis ting in Colorado. My heart breaks for our 'Merican cousins. Everyone lookin' for excuses an blame for dis horrible ting dat happen. Some people even sayin' if people were allowed to carry guns dis tragedy might be prevented. What??? I'm almos so speechless I can't even add "up with that?" Just "what???" To me dat's like sayin', "You know dat house wouldn't have burned down if they threw some gasoline on it." Boy oh boy. The right to bear arms should mean you get to wear T-shirts. Maybe dey need notwithstandin' clause in der constitution too. I doan know. So. Loonie game. Speakin' of loonies. You guys hear how Premier of Ontario Mike Harris wants to tes teachers evry 3 or 5 years to make sure dey're competent to teach. Good idea as long as we do dat for evrybody. Doctors. Lawyers. Politician. All of us could sit in a room, stadium maybe, an give premiers comptency tes. "Firs question. Are you still comin' up with bad ideas?" Well. Dat's unfair 'cause it's trick question, but sometimes little unfair is what government makes us do, too. So anyways, loonie game. Couple nights ago I'm in my ole home town, Ste. Rose du Lac. I got invite to nice dinner dey had for all der volunteers. An I tell you. Most amazin' tings start to happen. First most amazin' ting. I start rememberin' stuff. All kines of tings I forgot. Even saw my babysitter. I call her Ma Tante. Now I fine da kids she babysits today call her Mama. So I guess even with babysitters an nicknames der's some kine of hierarchy. An I visit peoples. Remember da house I used to live in. An eat. Boy did I eat. An den we all got to play da loonie game. Dis is a game where diffrent people put a loonie on da table an we passed it aroun an den we stopped. An da person with da loonie got to win da candle dat was sittin' on da table. An guess what. Dat was me. Boy at firs I was scared, 'cause I taught it was gonna be like da newcomer at bingos. Dey always seem to win an evrybody gets kine of mad at dem. But dat didn't happen dis time. After I won dat candle evrybody picked me up an put me on der shoulders an carried me aroun da room. Singing. OK well I'm 'saggerating. But I was so happy to win dat candle. It was lavender colour inside little jar with flowers on it. An den later on after evrybody said goodbye an went home. I was standin' der with da candle I jus won. Little message to me. To all of us. Shine dat light inside of you. Look for tings dat remine you how valuable you is. An how good life is. I went to my ole home an foun a piece of my past eh. Meetin' ole friens an new ones. Dose memries are little bit like our nose. Important part of who you are, but you forget about it so easily. So I'm glad I played da loonie game. Not 'cause I won a candle, but 'cause it remine me of who I am eh. Where I come from. I hope you guys fine little bits of your past today. Maybe someone you haven't talked to in years. Maybe visit where you have good memries you forget. Someting, anyting, that remines you despite all da loonieness in da world, life is good. I'm Joe from Winnipeg. Meegwetch.

Towels

Hey you guys, this is me, Joe from Winnipeg. Today I'm gonna be talkin' to you 'bout towels. But firs, are you guys ready to not buy da gasoline tomorrow. Big protes against da oil companies or somethin'. I heard one guy say, "It's not gonna work, 'cause we need our cars." Funny. How we accep dat statement, yet we hardly ever hear somebody sayin', I need my partner. Or I need my children. What's up with that? I doan know. Personal, I doan tink any of us needs cars. I'm talkin' 'bout towels 'cause I realized strange thing eh. I was invited to little gatherins at two seprate friens houses eh. So I go an dey're both pleasant events. An both of dem had one thing in common. Dey both used towels for curtains in da bathroom. In da both cases it wasn't too professional job eh. Dey jus sort of stuck dem on da window an stuffed dem into da little gap between da two parts of da window. Now I doan mean to be critical, but I got lots of experience hangin' tings in windows dat ain't supposed to be der eh. Like sheets. An even flags eh. I never had da kine dat was confederate flag or nothin' dough. Jus mosely da kine of flags dats from ole rock groups eh. One ting 'bout hangin' towels in da bathroom window I taught wasn't too bad idea was dat you could jus get out of da bath or da shower an der you go. You always got a towel der. Now dat would only be in case you didn't have dose towel hanger tings, which by da way I wish dey would make extra strength eh, 'cause I doan know how many of dose I've ripped off da wall tryin' to use dem for support. Anyways, I tink dat's good double use of a towel in da bathroom an as long as you be discrete anybody lookin' in on you would be disappointed eh. But dis get me thinkin' maybe we could use tings from da rooms where we live as tings to cover windows eh. Kine of like theme decoratin'. So you got bedsheets in da window in da bedroom. An couchcover or cushions in da livin' room. Tinfoil or da waxpaper in da kitchen. 'Cept I'm not too sure 'bout hallway near front door. You wouldn't get much privacy from a pair of boots or ole runners hangin' in dose windows. An I'm not sure 'bout nurseries. Diapers are kine of only good for one ting eh. An hey. You guys hear 'bout dis guy who invented new fire retard gel. It's made out of same stuff dey make diapers out of. He gets inspired by goin' to dump where dey're burnin' stuff an he notices dat diapers aren't burnin' eh. I'm kine of glad to know dose tings are indestructible eh, but why did dey need to make dem fire resist? So anyways dis guy figures, Hey. I'll make da fire retard gel out of dat. I'm glad he didn't tink of makin' house out of da diaper material eh. Or no-stick cookin' utensil. Or even firepeople's clothes. Dey do important job for us an I doan wanna picture dem slidin' down dat pole in diapers. Boy I guess I'm demonstratin' how dangerous it is when idea goes too far eh. But towels. People usin' towels as curtains makes me tink. Dis shows to me how resourceful we all are. I'm Joe from Winnipeg. Meegwetch.

Right Foot

Hey you guys, this is me, Joe from Winnipeg. Today I'm gonna be talkin' to you 'bout the right foot. Boy, what's up with all dese sleepin' giants eh. You notice how many of dem der is? Elections waiting to be called. Forest fires in Manitoba. Even my stomach eh. Dat's real sleepin' giant 'cause it growls whenever it wants somethin' eh. I'm thinkin' 'bout dose 'cause I hear der's sleepin' giant in Thunder Bay. Nanabijou it's called. I wanna go see dat some day. 'Cept my one frien Wally when I tole him dat, he says, "Why do you wanna go to Tundra Bay for? An leave sunny Winterpeg?" Ho ho. Dat's so original. I tink dese guys are jus jealous, 'cause I notice people always make fun of names of beautiful tings eh, people included. So. Right foot. I'm talkin' 'bout right foot 'cause dat's da one I know best. It was da foot I had hardest time gettin' right eh. Wait a minute. Anyways, when I was little kid an I had dose runners dat looked like slippers. 'Member dose. An yer mom would put a big "R" on der or an "L". Although I'm not sure why she did dat 'cause I didn't know how to read yet. An I kept puttin' dem on da wrong foot anyways. I tink of dat now an it's wonder I didn't get lost on my way to school eh. Or kept fallin' down all da time. Anyways, other night I'm stuck waitin' somewheres eh. An I'm waitin' der, thinkin' whether I should read da Poplar Mechanics from 1984. Or if I should count da hair on my arms. An den dis woman sits down eh. Normally dat's not a big deal, but I look at her foot 'cause I thought dere was a spider on der eh. An I notice dat she's wearin' dose slipper kine of runners dat I used to wear. An what I thought was spider is a little drawin' of an angel. Hmm. Dat's intrestin' I thought. An I look at other foot an der's a heart drawn on der. I was wondrin' why dis woman had drawings on her feet eh. Maybe she walked with her head down all da time. Or maybe she wanted a logo dat meant somethin' eh. Or else maybe she jus wanted to be remineded dat dere's someone lookin' after her, an love too, eh. Dat's what I like to tink 'cause right foots always make me tink of my mom eh. Me sittin' on da bed. Her holdin' my slipper runner, sayin' "Push. Push Joe. Don't kick dis time." An yeah, you could say moms are angels too, but right foots also remine me dat sometimes moms give us good kick in da pants when we need it eh. Sometimes a warm handshake. I'm just kiddin'. If yer shakin' hands with yer mom instead of huggin' her you should talk a little bit. I know some of us have hard times with our mothers. Me included. Maybe dat's so da analyst can have somethin' to analyze. "How do you feel 'bout yer mother?" "Great." "Come on now. You can tell me." "No. Really. Great." "Ohhh." But I tink it's 'cause our mothers are people too, eh. It's easy to forget dat. But however you spen Mother's Day, whether dat's takin' her out to get a big flower to put on her dress an a nice meal, or free cake from one of da chicken places, or maybe even jus a nice walk outside, I hope it starts out on da right foot. An if it starts on da left, stop an start again. This is Joe from Winnipeg. Meegwetch.

Strawberry Lifesavers

Hey you guys, this is me, Joe from Winnipeg. Today I'm gonna be talkin' to you 'bout strawberry Lifesavers, and Winston Churchill too, a little bit. Hey, you guys see the da Toronto newspaper we got in Winnipeg? Boy, dat's good, 'cause I tink Toronto's kine of like fibre, always need more of it in my life eh. I'm just kidding. I tink I'm just lashin' out 'cause I do dat when I'm nervous. I been seein' strange tings, like Prime Minister Chrétien playin' basketball, an he was doin' real good and den he fell, scratched up his hans. Fallin's definitely not good for politicians eh, look what happened to Gerald Ford. Dat whole fallin' ting dough was 'cause of one ting. He was wearin' da wrong shoes. You don't play basketball in oxfords eh. An what's up with dis Sheila Copps. She changed her hair. Looks good, but I doan ting she should be usin' Preston Manning as an Obi Wan Kenobi. Ha. You thought you'd get away without a *Star Wars* refrence? Forget it. Anyways, 'member when Manning changed his hair, I believed he was a completely diffrent person. Hey. Where'd dat other guy go? Who are you? You mus be "kinder and gentler" 'cause now you got hair like Elvis. OK. Dat's enough. Anyways, strawberry Lifesavers. Oh yeah, and Winston Churchill. See. I figured somethin' out about Canadians da other day. What it is about us an who we are. See, when I was little boy der was a girl I liked eh. So I gave her bran new strawberry Lifesavers as present. But two other of my friens saw me do dis. So I had to give dem strawberry Lifesavers too, so dat dey wouldn't know I liked dis girl. Boy, what a mess, dat was costin' me an extra 70 cents a week eh. An I was reminded of dis when I saw newspaper other day talkin' 'bout how much Winston Churchill liked Canada eh. Basically it was sayin' how we mus be valid as a country 'cause Winston Churchill liked us. An den I realized dat's da ting about us Canadians eh. We want to be liked. At all costs. An dat's natural human desire, to be liked. But if your not careful it can get to be like da strawberry Lifesavers eh. You start doin' silly tings. An you start denying tings too. Der's lots dat's good about Canada eh, but der's also lots dat needs work. An I sometimes tink we're a little bit too ready to deny dat eh. "Oh dat's not a problem. How 'bout dose Jets?" Dey're gone actually. "Oh yes, well…hmmm." I'm not tryin' to bum you guys out or anythin', 'cause der's so many good ways to start a day eh. I'm jus sayin' dat whatever you do in yer lives, make sure it's da right ting for you. An yer not doin' somethin' jus to be liked. Dat might end up costin' you 70 cents extra a week. Jus be

yer TRUE self an you'll fine people'll be givin' you strawberry Lifesavers. I'm Joe from Winnipeg. Meegwetch.

A Little Dog Wearin' Nail Polish

Hey you guys, this is me, Joe from Winnipeg. Today I'm gonna be talkin' to you 'bout a little dog wearin' naipolish. Get to that in a sec. You guys hear dey're talkin' 'bout floods again. All over da place, in the north an south an in our basements. Boy, I'm glad I doan live in a basement no more. It was bad enough tryin' to get some sleep with people thumpin' aroun on top of you without havin' to worry 'bout flooding. An I know lots of you is worryin' right now. I'm sure der's better tings to do dan dat, but I know if I was in yer place I'd do da same ting. So, little dog wearin' nail polish. What's up with that? I was usin' a payphone the other day eh. An I was listenin' to the computer or whoever dat was. You know how dey trick us into tinkin' we're gonna get to talk to somebody. I really miss talkin' to people when I use da phone now. Anyways, da phone's sayin' to me, "If you know da name of da person you wish to speak to, please enter dat. Followed by number sign." So then I start spellin' with numbers I guess T O M what's his name, but it says "No such person." Oh, I was gettin' so frustrated eh.

'Cause I couldn't remember Tom's last name. So I started guessin'. I was typin' all kines of numbers an names in there, sometimes even talkin' to people, some of dem even sayin' "How'd you get dis number? You're not s'posed to be actually talkin' to anybody." So jus as I'm about to give up dis woman stands beside me an ties up her little dog to the payphone beside me eh. An she talks to him an says "Now you be good an don't go nowhere." I like how people assume dogs speak English eh. Maybe dey speak German. Or Chinese, who knows. Anyways, da dog looks real scared, so I figure I better not touch it. An I look at its little nails eh, well actually they were kine of big for a little dog. An I got bad flashback eh, of little dogs nails on linoleum. You know how that souns? Tsk tsk tsk tsk tsk. Ho. Anyways, I look closer an I see dis little dog's got nail polish on. Kine of bubblegum coloured. What's up with that? I'm tinkin'. An right away I start judgin' dat little dog, tinkin' dat's not right. You shouldn't be wearin' dat. Other dogs won't be carin' 'bout what shade nail polish you got. Or even dat you got nail polish. Boy, I was so shocked I even forgot to hang up the payphone. I just walked away. Den I was tinkin', why is dis botherin' me. Dat little dog wasn't doin' nothin' to me. It didn't even know itself dat some-body put nail polish on it. Or snipped its tail. Or put dose funny tings on its ears to make dem stick up straight. Here I was judgin' it just 'cause I wouldn't do dat. Or it offended my idea of how dog's is s'posed to be treated. Den I get a little scared and sad eh. 'Cause I realize dat I'm not alone. Dere's lots of people who judge each others. An say you shouldn't be doin' dat. Or dis. Or you're livin' wrong. Or I'm livin' right. I tink maybe dat little dog with the nail polish's doin' a good ting eh. Mindin' his own business. Livin' for nice walks. An crunchy food, occasional steak bone in der. Jus bein' hisself. Livin' an let live eh. I'm Joe from Winnipeg. Meegwetch.

Alphabet Letters

Hey you guys, this is me, Joe from Winnipeg. Today I'm gonna be talkin' to you 'bout alphabet letters. Very specific ones actually. I say alphabet letters 'cause I don't wanna confuse you guys today. I'm findin' there's way too much confusion in da world. Even people bein' confused about bein' confused. Oh yeah, I almos forgot. My frien is turnin' 50, so dey're kind of depressed, 'cause now dey won't be on da 6/49 draw no more eh. Dey could always pick one of da numbers for how old dey are. But I really tink dey're upset about somethin' else eh. Realizin' dey're prob'ly never gonna win 6/49. You know, I heard somebody say dat lotteries is a tax on da poor. An another guy sayin' lotteries is a tax on da stupid. I'm glad somebody 'xplained dat to me. 'Cause I was wondrin' why I was gettin' taxed so high eh. But part of dat definition don't work 'cause if taxes was voluntary like lottery dis country'd be broke right now. So. Alphabet letters. Da specific ones I'm talkin' 'bout today is P. R. V. and S. But not in dat order. Da order I saw dem in was R. S. V. and P. Some guy I know's gettin' married eh. An he hans me dis invitation thing. Says to me, "I know it's a week late, but just show up anyways." "Oh tank you," I says, an I take dis invitation. I look on der an I see dat it says R.S.V. and P by such an such date. But I'm not sure what dis is eh. 'Cause in my famly we never did dis. You jus showed up an ate Chicken Delight an hit da glasses with yer spoon to make da couple kiss. An you do the big line thing where you shake hans an smooch da bridesmaids. I know dis R.S.V. an P ting is French eh. Dat's prob'ly why I'm intimidated. I'm scared of offending somehow. So I doan know what to do eh. So I phone my cousin Erin an ask her what to do. An den I realize, too late, what if she's not invited. Now I'm offending anyways, but it was OK. An she was invited. So she says to me, "I doan know. We always just expect people to show up. Or else just tell them to be there." An you know, dat's right eh. An I know these alphabet letters in dis order mean, "let me know if you're coming", but it's just funny how silly we get sometimes eh. Tings like weddings an those bar mitsvahs an birthdays, oh what are we gonna do? I doan wanna offend anyone. Scared to mess up a tradition instead of maybe makin' a new one. The ting I come to see is dat all dat matters is dat we show up. Take part in whatever tradition or ritual people are creatin' eh. Bein' a part of somethin' bigger than us all. An dis guy who asked me to R.S.V. an P don't know me too well. 'Cause anythin' where someone's gonna feed me…I'll be right dere. I'm Joe from Winnipeg. Meegwetch.

Ropes

Hey you guys, this is me, Joe from Winnipeg. Today I'm gonna be talkin' to you 'bout ropes. Dat can be a big metaphor so I'll take it easy. But you ever wonder what dat means, "learnin' the ropes"? It don't really make sense. What's dis rope? Nylon. Dis one? Uhmmm, plain rope. An what about "on da ropes." Or "a rope in da hand can burn your hand if yer climbin' it an slip." Or what about dat Alfred Hitchcock movie, *Rope*. I like dat guy's movies. Even dat one, *Psycho*. I tink he was ahead of his time on dat one though, 'cause I hear people gettin' called dat all da time. So anyways, rope. I been tinkin' 'bout rope for a couple reasons. Da other day my dad was tellin' me a story 'bout how him an his brother had to milk cows eh. I always wanted to do dat but I'm afraid I wouldn't be able to get it into the cartons too good. So anyways, my dad tells me dey used to let the calf have some milk and then dey would pull it away an start milkin' the mama cow. Anyways, after a little while dis calf starts gettin' bigger eh. An harder an harder to pull away. So dat one day dey can't even move it eh. So my dad an his brother get da bright idea to tie some rope under da cow's legs or arms or whatever an pull it away from its mama so dey could get some milk too. Anyways, dey do dis an end up liftin' da little calf up into da air. So dey milk da cow an let da calf down. 'Cept it can't stand up now eh, 'cause the circulation got cut off. Boy, were dey ever scared. So dey tell deir mom, my granny, 'bout da calf an she freaks out an calls her brother who was da local vetrinary guy. An he can't figure it out an pretty soon dere's all dese people scared of some new disease dat might be happenin' to the cows. An all the while my dad an my uncle are not sayin' nothin'. Dey're too scared. But dey never used a rope like dat again eh. So as I'm tinkin' this story I see dis little train of kids walkin' down da street. An dey're all holdin' a rope eh. An I tink dat's a good idea. Keep dem together so dey all get to da same place at da same time. An den I 'member da only time I ever used a rope was for tug o' war eh. I always wanted to be da anchor person, but dere was somethin' 'bout bein' at da end of a rope, makin' a knot an den just hangin' on dat I didn't like. Plus I wasn't strong enough. But dat tug o' war's kine of a perfect game for us human bein's. We seem to be doin' dat all da time, pullin' against each others an not gettin' nowheres eh. But da thing 'bout all these ropes is dey're connectin' us somehow eh. Remindin' us we're all connected, too. Even helpin' us help each other. Whether dat's liftin' up cows. Or keepin' little ones safe. Or even playin' a game. I hope you guys have all da ropes you need, literal an figural eh. I'm Joe from Winnipeg. Meegwetch.

Odometer Checks

Hey you guys, this is me, Joe from Winnipeg. Today I'm gonna be talkin' to you 'bout odometer checks. I had to go drive somebody to Moosomin, Saskatchewan eh. You guys ever been der? Nice place. Anyways, after my frien picked up der cheque I drove dem back to Winnipeg 'cause dey always feel safer on da highway if somebody else is drivin'. I guess dat flattered me, 'cause I'm used to my passengers grabbin' da dash board and movin' der leg like dey're pushin' a brake. So anyways, we're drivin' home an my frien falls asleep. An I don't got much to do except drive an tink. I didn't turn on da radio 'cause I didn't want to wake up my frien. An we're drivin' along da Trans Canada an I'm tinkin' 'bout things. Gettin' all contem plative. Or is it contemplative. I'm never sure 'bout dat. So I contemplated dat question for a while. An den I pass dis sign dat says odometer check, one kilo-metre. An den another sign. Begin odometer check now. An for some reason I got paranoid eh. It was just like I was takin' a test instead of a check. An I'm drivin' an tryin' to make sure da odometer's rollin' past da same number as I pass da signs dat say one kilometre. Or is it kilometre. Don't get distracted Joe. Two kilometre. An so on. An I see dat da seven comes up at about da same time for evry sign, but I'm not too sure 'cause I was tryin' to watch da road an da number an da sign at da same time eh. It was VERY hard eh. An boy, if I didn't start contemplatin' life eh. An dat's what dat odometer check is like. 'Cept da signs doan say kilometre so an so. Dey're tings like baby's bein' born. Graduatin' things. Maybe even doctor checkup eh. Any little time we look aroun an go, "Yup. I doan really know what I'm doin'. But everythin seems OK." An it's always good to check an make sure yer life is goin' the way you want it to. 'Cause if it isn't, you're the driver. 'Member that. An for me, the thing I contempl...thought about was how come I'm so lucky dat I get to talk to you peoples evry week. I'm just a guy. An der's lots of peoples with da same ideas, even better ones. All I can tink is, I'm s'posed to be doin' dis. You know, for a long time Native people have had to struggle to be heard. Lots of us are still tryin' to find our voice eh. How do we get heard? Are people listenin'? An I have to say yes. Some people are listenin'. An some people are doin' like da odometer checks on all of us all da time eh. How come dese people are hungry? How come dey're still so much war? What are we doin' about this? 'Cause thing I noticed too 'bout dose odometer checks. We doan really need dem. What if yer odometer don't work? Are you gonna stop yer car on da highway, get out an walk away? "Oh no. I can't ride in dat car. Da odometer don't work." It's just a good reminder for us dat sometimes tings need attendin' too. I'm Joe from Winnipeg. Meegwetch.

Lords

Hey you guys, this is me, Joe from Winnipeg. Today I'm gonna be talkin' to you 'bout lords. I wanna be a lord. Don't you guys wanna be lords? I'm not even sure what dat is, but I tink it souns cool. It's kine of neutral, too. So you could be a good person or a bad person an still be a lord. You'd even get to go to parties. An der would be big steps der an trumpets, an dey'd announce you. Announcin' Lord Joe. Or whatever your name is. 'Cept then I'd become like the chef on *Sesame Street* who would say somethin' like, 10 chocolate cakes. An then oof uff ow an he'd fall down da stairs tryin' to carry too much. Dat's probably what happens when you get too many titles. You start to fall down. Ahh well, don't matter anyways, I doan tink any of us'll get to be lords 'cause Canada's dis classless society eh. But I doan tink many of us will get to be lords 'cause if da supposed real reason Mr. Black doesn't get to be a lord is 'cause he criticized Chrétien, den not many of us would get any honours eh. But da other reason I want to talk to you guys 'bout lords is 'cause it's supposed to be an honour eh.

An I been tinkin' 'bout honours lately 'cause it's dat season when lots of young peoples are graduatin'. An dat's a real honour. For you. An yer famly eh. For some of yous yer finely finishin' 12 or more years of school. An for some of yous yer just startin' 12 or more years of post-secondary education. Da one ting I gotta say, well actually I always say more dan one ting, but I gotta remine you is to try an be humble. I know it's hard if yer winnin' lots of rewards an you get to be da validictatorian. An you can teach a lesson to da other grads, like maybe the one 'bout da rabbit and da turtle. Where da rabbit falls asleep an da turtle wins da race. I'm not all crazy 'bout dat lesson though, 'cause in some ways it's sayin' most of us is turtles, slow, probably gonna lose, an the only way we can win is if da real fast guys fall asleep. I'm prob'ly just jealous I never got to be the valedictatorian, that was 'cause my mortar board didn't fit an I had bad grades, but den too, maybe dat's why I try an teach lessons to you guys now. I'm tryin' to fulfill dat unfulfilled dream of not bein' valedictatorian. Anyways, dat's what you guys got ahead of yous. Lots of dreams. An a beautiful summer. Hey some of yous might even get a car for your grad present. I was always jealous of dose guys, but I got a grad present, too. I got da honour of makin' people proud. My friens, my famly, myself. An dat's da real honour eh. An you guys who didn't graduate yet: doan worry. You will. Or you can. Funny ting 'bout life, seems like yer always graduatin'. I'm Joe from Winnipeg. Meegwetch.

Canada

Hey you guys, this is me, Joe from Winnipeg. Today I'm gonna be talkin' to you 'bout Canada. I know I'm usehly more vague in da tings I talk about, but den Canada's little bit vague sometimes so... Anyways, I was sittin' around contemplatin' my cereal an milk eh. Like, how much milk is enough milk for cereal. Just a little bit, so da cereal dominates, or maybe a whole bunch so dat da cereal's floatin' eh. Or should you have enough milk so dere's some left to drink out of da bowl afterwards? An what if it's Fruit Loops, den da milk gets discoloured an more milky. Is dat possible? Milky milk. Souns like some kine of rapper. Anyways, as I was contemplatin' my milk cereal ratios I was readin' the box an at first I thought it said "...if this product does not have enough meat for your expectations..." an I got kine of mad eh. Hey, they're rippin' us consumers off, there's no meat in this cereal. Den I thought, wait a minute, dat's a good thing. So I read it again an saw that it was "meet" with two e's, not an a eh. Den I'm tinkin' dat's a good ting I caught my mistake otherwise I would have been at the grocery store with my Corn Flakes sayin' "Where's the beef?" But I was able to avoid dis huge misunderstandin' by double checkin' an applying some logic. So dat's what started me thinkin' 'bout Canada. 'Cause dis whole country got its name from a misunderstandin' eh. I'm sure most of you know dis story where dey first come to Turtle Island an ask the 'Nishnawbe what dis land is called, an they say, "Kanata". An da rest is a history. I mean, "an" history. Der's been misunderstandin' goin' on before dis nation was here eh. An it's still goin' on today. Between diffrent peoples. 'Specially between the 'Nishnawbe an da rest of Canada. Nurses. All kines of workers actually. Misunderstandin' in famlies. Between friens. You name it. But I believe we're gonna work dat out. We'll fine just da right mix of da milk an da cereal. Maybe realize dat it's all a matter of personal taste anyways. I hope you guys avoid misunderstandin' in yer life today. An have a good time in dis wonderful country dat maybe should have had a diffrent name, but den again, it works. Have a good summer. I'm Joe from Winnipeg. Meegwetch.

Plastic

Hey you guys, this is me, Joe from Winnipeg. Today I'm gonna be talkin' to you 'bout a big piece of plastic. I gotta do dat 'cause I wasn't sure what to talk about at first. Der's so much goin' on. But den der's always so much goin' on. I guess dis time my ole big mouth could only say so much eh. So. OK. Big mouth. Do yer stuff. Happy Birthday Winnipeg. I know some peoples wanted a big party or a cake, but I tink dat Winnipeg is actin' how most of us get when we get older eh. Jus rather forget about da birthdays. Preten der just another day. I doan know, but to me, celebratin' community's a good ting. An I love dat I can say dat I'm Joe from "Winnipeg". Joe from someplace else would make me feel lost eh. We got a new L-G too, eh. I'm tryin' to make dat soun more hip. I doan really know what a leftenant is. But I know what a governor is. Maybe some day we'll have a wrestler for our leftenant governor. Boy, den if I got to meet him he might give me a body slam instead of da hand shake. An say, "Der, is dat fake? Hunh?" I'm just kidding. An den der's da Clinton. You know dat whole mess jus proves one ting. We're always our own worse enemy eh. Whether dat's a country. Or us individuals. An den all da pain an war in da Kosovo. You jus wanna cry an go, "What's up with dat?" An dis guy who buried hisself under da groun for 150 days or something. Livin' der with a TV an not much else. Dey call him da human mole. Dose English peoples is so polite. I know housin's always a problem, but why would you want to live in a box? What would ole Edgar Allen Poe tink eh? An da new smokin' labels. Maybe dey should jus put a big ole dead rat on der with a circle an a line through him. Warning. Poison. SO. Big piece of plastic. I was watchin' dis big piece of plastic stuck in a tree eh. It was twisted aroun part of it. An other parts were held by da branches. An once in a while da wind would catch it eh. An puff it out like da back of our jackets on a windy day. An I thought boy, dat ting is tryin' to escape from dat tree. But it prob'ly won't never happen. An den I thought, boy, dat big piece of plastic's kine of like us eh. We're held together by many tings. It's all very complex. An sometimes der's lots goin' on. An it's all very excitin'. An other times it's all relax eh. Jus like all da stuff dat's goin' on. Rise an fall kine of. But da funny ting about watchin' dis big piece of plastic an tinkin' it's kine of like us an our lives. Big an small. Da ting we're tryin' to get away from is what's holdin' us together. Very strange dat. Boy. I'm even gonna mix up da metaphor an say dat we're da tree too eh. Our community. Our histry. But da ting I noticed most about dis big piece of plastic in a tree was how beautiful it was eh. I'm Joe from Winnipeg. Meegwetch.

Man who buried himself .... human interest
new Lieutenant Governor .... politics
Clinton impeachment .... politics
Slurpee straw .... food
Tobacco .... health
Kosovo .... war
Winnipeg's birthday .... politics

Bagpipes

Hey you guys, this is me, Joe from Winnipeg. Today I'm gonna be talkin' to you 'bout bagpipes. I'm wantin' to be more useful to you guys, so here are the unofficial losing lottery results. Jus about evry ticket out der. An for mos of us who play lottery. One out of six numbers right. I gotta admit I doan usehly buy tickets eh. Only if I get dat funny feelin' when I'm walkin' by the ticket seller and den I go spen my dollar and den I lose. Maybe dat feelin' I'm gettin' really means I shouldn't be buyin' dose tickets in da firs place. I also foun out dat da green plastic garbage bag was co-invented by a Winnipeger named Harry Wasyluk. Meegwetch to you, Harry. You helped make our kitchens less smelly an also gave us someting you can carry clothes in or make a raincoat out of. An it also keeps us unconfused about garbage. Nobody's goin', "Hey what's in that green plastic bag? Maybe it's treasure." So I was hearin' the news with dis other earthquake dat happened in da Colombia eh. More bad news, but der was somethin' der dat warmed my heart eh. I heard dem say dat disaster relief teams from Japan an USA was goin' der to help. An dat's good. Dat der's people in the world whose only job is to help other people in need. So anyways, bagpipes. I been tinkin' 'bout bagpipes lately eh. I got dis one bagpipe song stuck in my head. Don't you hate when dat happens. You're mindin' yer own business an den all of a sudden you hear "Da Bonny Lass of Fyvie" in yer head. An den you can pas dat tune on too eh. Kine of like a yawn dat way. I tink I got bagpipes an bagpipe songs in my head 'cause of dat guy who got charged eh. Dey charged him with "willfully damaging bagpipes". What's up with that? Der must be a charge for unwillfully damaging bagpipes too, eh. An I can unerstand why somebody would willfully damage bagpipes sometimes, too. But what if you say accidently walked by the bagpipe player an you tripped or something an you hit the drones an den the bagpipe player would go, "Hey. Dat's charges." Boy. I'm gonna be extra careful aroun dose guys now. I always was afraid of dem. Now I jus got more reason eh. But da other ting I've been realizin' 'bout bagpipes is dat dey're very ole eh. Dey're an ancient instrument. An I foun dat out from my frien Jenny, who's prob'ly sittin' in her car right now somewhere. Dat da bagpipes are da national instrument of Scotland. Dat's pretty cool. But den it gets me tinkin'. What's Canada's national instrument? Maybe it's somethin' obscure like the kazoo. Or else what if it's say a French horn. But den I can't see English people puttin' up with dat. Maybe it's a viola or an oboe. Harpsichord too, maybe. 'Cept for me, if we doan got a national instrument yet. I think we should make it a drum eh. Somethin' dat speaks to all of us. Somethin' you can dance to. An somethin' every people in da world seem to have invented. I tink music is somethin' we can't get enough of in our lives eh. Unless maybe it's a bagpipe song stuck in yer head. I'm Joe from Winnipeg. Meegwetch.

Who's the Boss?

Hey you guys, this is me, Joe from Winnipeg. Today I'm gonna be talkin' to you 'bout who's de boss. I doan mean dat sitcom with da Tony Danza an Judith Light. Da one where he was an old taxi driver who was her maid or someting like dat. Didn't really make sense, 'cause you jus knew dat she was da boss. So I doan know how come dey had a question mark on da title. Boy. Did you guys see da sunset da other night? I jus looked like somebody asked me how to fix a broken water main. My mouth was hangin' open. My eyes blinked a couple times. It was beautiful blues an greens an some other colour I doan know how to say. Anyways, I was standin' der an my frien Howie walks past me eh. Mumbling somethin'. Completely ignoring me. An he's holding somethin' in his han. Lookin' at it. So I go to ask Howie what he's doin', an I hear him sayin', "Looks like plastic. But it feels like rubber." "What does?" I ask him. An he shows me dis little ting he's holdin'. So I takes it an I go. "Hmmm. Does look like plastic an feel like rubber. Where'd you get it?" "My nose." he tells me. Ahhh. I'm jus kidding. But it was my frien Howie. An we tell each other all da excitin' things happenin' in our lives. "What's new with you?" "Nothin'. How 'bout you?" "Same." An den Howie says. "Oh. Der is somethin' new. My boss left us." An I ask him what he means, an den he tells me dat his boss jus took off. So who's da boss I ask him. An he says he don't know. But he's kine of scared, 'cause without a hierarchichal structure at work he's afraid there's gonna be too many liberties. I tole him not to worry dough. It's pretty hard to tink of liberties an workin' for da government. But you know. All dis worryin' 'bout who's da boss makes me tink 'bout dis Wantonio Sam-a-ranch. Boy, I have a hard time with dat guy's name. I wish he had a "ma" at da en of his name instead of a "nch", den he'd be Wantonio Samarama. Now I hear he had an extravaganza in da Japan. It could've been da Samarama 'Stravaganza. An dey cooked da expense books in Nagano. Real literal eh. Dey burned dem 'cause dey say dey didn't have no place to put dem. Boy, I fine dat one hard to buy, dat's when garbage bags come in handy as storage containers. Speakin' of buy, I guess dat's what started dis whole ting. Buyin' da 'Lympics. An IOC people. I doan even know what dat IOC is. An when I wonder who's da boss, I know it's dat Samaranch guy. I tink people want him to just take off too, eh. But why should he? He can jus say what my nephew says when I tell him to go to bed, "You're not da boss of me." An I usehly scratch my head an tink "he's right." I guess da one ting I learned 'bout dis whole 'Lympic scandal ting is we all got a boss eh. An dat's us.

Next time someone asks you "who's da boss aroun here?" you can say, "me." I just wish dis Sam-a-ranch guy, who already knows he's da boss, would use dat power for good, instead of tryin' blow smoke with dis new duping commission. Me, I'm gonna go look at da sky again to remine myself dat der's an even bigger boss over all of us eh. (Da weather.) I'm Joe from Winnipeg. Meegwetch.

Sittin'

Hey you guys, this is me, Joe from Winnipeg. Today I'm gonna be talkin' to you 'bout sittin'. But first. You know what I hate? I hate when you buy a piece of meat. Like say a smoked weiner, which you might enjoy eatin' raw. Dey're good dat way an make a satisfyin', almos crunchy sound when you eat dem. I know only chocolate bars an apples are s'posed to be crunchy, but I doan know what else to call it. Anyways, I hate when you forget to rewrap yer piece of meat in dat funny baloney-coloured paper. An you go to da fridge lookin' for dat special smoked weiner dat you saved an you realize dat you left it on da counter. Unwrapped. An den you look. An da parts of da smoked weiner dat was stickin' out are all brown. Not dat funny baloney colour like da paper. Den you got to eat aroun da parts of da smoked weiner dat ain't brown. An dey're wasted. Just wasted. You got to throw dem out. I thought I might boil dat weiner but I doan know. I was wondrin' why meat dat's left out changes like dat. Can't be good for you. But den I guess eatin' raw smoked weiners ain't good for you neither.

Anyways. So. Sittin'. I ran into my frien Debra. I almos didn't reconize her 'cause she was walkin' with her head down, comin' towards me on dat little trail dat's in da deep snow 'fore dey snowplow da sidewalk. I say meegwetch to you guys who have to be da trailblazers goin' to work in da mornin'. Makin' dat little path for da rest of us. 'Cause der's no reason we should all get snow in our boots. Anyways, I almos bumped into my frien 'cause neither of us was steppin' off da little trail. We both had short shoes on eh. I like how people can lose der manners when it comes to gettin' der feet wet. Anyways, we reconized each other an talked. I asked her how come she had her head down an she said she was just worryin'. As useshwal. An den I said, "Worryin' is just misused imagination." An she liked dat. Taught I was "wise". An I tole her I read it on a billboard. But she still liked it. So I asked what she was worryin' 'bout. An she tole me dat she's been sittin' aroun for too long. Not doin' da tings she wants to. An how maybe she should be an MLA for Manitoba 'cause dey get paid for sittin'. Although I tink it's been a lots a months since dey've been sittin'. Kine of scary dat da government seems to chug along even dough der's been nobody in da legislature for almost a year. What's up with dat? But I thought about dat. Sittin'. Dreamin' up jobs where I might get paid while I sit. Security guard maybe. Truck driver. Some kine of writer. It's still all hard work eh. Which I doan mine, but me, just like lots of people, got da fantasy dat we should just get paid. You know, some of us spend lots of our lives sittin'. Some of it good, like visitin' each others. Or else eatin' yer breakfast listenin' to da radio. Some not so good, like too much TV. Or even maybe some of da tings we need to do in our lives eh. Like goin' to da doctor for a checkup maybe. Or takin' dose singin' lessons you want. Or callin' yer frien you haven't spoke to in real long. Sittin' can be good for restin', but comes der da time we gotta get up an do somethin'. Like me. Right now. I'm goin' to buy more smoked weiners. This is Joe from Winnipeg. Meegwetch.

Iciness

Hey you guys, this is me, Joe from Winnipeg. Today I'm gonna be talkin' to you 'bout bubble gum. I was gonna talk 'bout false alarms, but there's been too many of dose already. You guys know dat if you get more dan one false alarm you gotta pay 75 bucks? What's up with dat? How come politicians don't get charged 75 bucks for false alarms? Poor old Glen Clarke would be in trouble. Or wait. Dat's false budget. So anyways, bubble gum. I figured I'd talk 'bout bubble gum 'cause I been havin' run-ins with it lately eh. I foun some on my shoe. An it was the kine dat's jus da right consistence to make a mess eh. Even sticking to da stick I was usin' to get rid of it. Boy, den too, I even dropped a penny in da restraunt an went lookin' for it eh, in case it was one of dose '43 pennies dat's brown. I thought all pennies was brown. It's good to know though dat things from 1943 is still valuable. But boy, you should've seen under dat table. Looked like a little bubble gum colony under der. All growin' in diffrent colours. Hard as rocks too, 'cause I bumped my head on some of dat bubble gum when I got up. Reminded me of my frien Thomas. Dat guy used to recycle dat bubble gum from under da desks at school eh. I was always surprised he could make dat bubble gum chewable again. Never broke a tooth neither. Anyways, I ran into my frien Debra again. Sittin' on da bench waitin' for da bus. "Hey what's up with you?" I said to her. "Not much. You want some gum?" An she offered me some of da new Slurpee flavour bubble gum from da Sev eh. Dat's not open I tole her. You should have da first piece for yourself. Den she tells me she don't chew gum eh. Never has in her whole life. Always 'fraid she'd choke. An tole me she couldn't unerstand da concept of chewin' somethin' like dat for so long an not gettin' nothin' out of it. I tole her she should try my cookin'. I make da baloney as sof as boiled leather. Anyways. I asked her how come she bought gum if she wasn't gonna chew it. An she tole me she was going to give it a try. Jus for a change. But den she changed her mine an bought Tic Tacs. An how come dose tings aren't jus da tic or da tac eh. Dey're all da same candy. It should just be tics. Or tacs. Although I guess neither of dose sounds tasty. Anyways, my frien Debra got me tinkin' 'bout bubble gum an change eh. How dat bubble gum can be like situations in our life. We jus keep chewin' it till we should stick it under da table, but some of us don't. We keep chewin'. Even dough der's no flavour der. An how sometimes it can get sticky eh. Real mess. I been noticin' lately how so many peoples are going through change eh. An how so many of us try to avoid it. Which is even more weirder 'cause most of us seem to want it all da time. Den when we get it, we don't want it. What's up with that? Only ting I know for sure is change is gonna happen. In lots of ways. I'm Joe from Winnipeg. Meegwetch.

Intrest

Hey you guys, this is me, Joe from Winnipeg. Today I'm gonna be talkin' to you 'bout intrest. But firs thing, you guys hear dat story 'bout how people in da world stopped fighting each other for da same reason dey're fighting in da firs place? Jus because. Nope. Me neither. But one day we're gonna hear it. So anyways, intrest. Well. I was in da sporting good store da other day eh, 'cause I needed to buy myself a bran new ball. Any kine. I went der with open mine. I thought, Joe you buy what ever kine of ball you want. Basket. Foot. Red and blue with white stripe. Boy, even da fame Super Ball. Da kine dat would bounce REALLY high. I figured I needed to buy somethin' to have fun wit. An nex to yo yo a ball is my favrit toy. So der I was lookin' for da kine of ball I was gonna buy, an you know what? Dey package dem in boxes. What's up with dat? I'd rather dey jus let dem be free. I even picture da delivry truck driver opening up da back of his truck an balls bouncin' everywhere. So, while I'm der mutterin' to myself dis guy comes up to me an says, "'Scuse me. I'm intrested in findin' out where da pickrel rigs are." An I says, "Oh I doan work here. But dey're prob'ly in da fishin' section." An den he gives me one of dose looks dat says, "Like duhh. Hello? I already looked der." An I 'pologize little bit, but we get talkin'. I fine out his name's Rod from Thompson. An I ask him why he's intrested in buyin' pickrel rigs so early eh. He tells me he jus findly got his skidoo fixed an now all da snow is meltin'. What's up with dat? Rod tells me you can't get started too early when it comes to gettin' ready for fishin'. An he tells me dis story 'bout how he caught six pickrels on da one pickrel rig once eh. I didn't want to call 'tention to his fish story eh. But I tried real hard in myself to believe dat story. Den he tole me 'bout da fish he caught dat had another fish inside it an dat fish had another one inside it an so on. I tink he said der was 'bout ten fishes inside each other. Boy, dis time I jus had to say, "OK. Sure. You're startin' to soun like Jean Chrétien now." I tell him. "What do you mean?" he says to me. An I say, dat guy's been tellin' da biggest fish stories in all of Canada. So den we get into political discussion eh. We debate little bit 'bout conflic of intrest. An how we heard da prime minister talkin' an sayin' he had no intrest in dat hotel. Hmmm. Souns like der's lots of tings he's not intrested in eh. All da labour unrest in dis country. Human rights over pay equity. Brian Mulroney turnin' sixty. Well I guess we can't blame him for dat last one. I doan know too many people intrested in dat either. But you know, even dough der's all dis bad news we hear about, I guess 'cause we're all s'posed to be intrested in it, I'm still glad. I'm glad in dat life gives us many tings we can choose to express intrest eh. Whether dat's a hobby of workin' with balsa wood or square dancin' to expressin' intrest in our work, maybe wit other people, maybe in business, you name it. Even me an old Rod. He's got intrest in fishin' an pickrel rigs. An I got intrest in playin' wit da football I bought. I picked dat one 'cause you need two people for it to work right. I hope you guys have lots of intrest today, whether dats intrest in yer famly or even yer bank account. I'm Joe from Winnipeg. Meegwetch.

Screwballs

Hey you guys, this is me, Joe from Winnipeg. Today I'm gonna be talkin' to you 'bout screwballs. Boy, der's just so many screwballs I doan know where to begin. Let's start with da goverment. Aenhh. I'm just kidding. Dat's not da kine of screwballs I mean. Although der's sure plenty out der. Take yer pick eh. I kine of like da word 'cause it's not too mean eh. You can call somebody a screwball an it's little bit compliment. "Hey. You know what? Yer a screwball. I can't believe you did dat." An dey might smile an nod der head an say, "Yup. dat's me. Screwball." People like bein' risky without bein' called da real negative names eh. An hey. Speakin' of dat. I doan usheally do dis, but I gotta say someting. It's botherin' me too much. You know dis horrible, awful, messy ting dat's goin' on in da Kosovo. An sometimes I hear da newspeople usin' da words "ethnic cleansing". I wish dey wouldn't do dat, 'cause dey're instillin' dose thoughts in people's heads. Like dat's what's goin' on. "Ethnic cleansing". It's murder you guys. An genocide. Not "ethnic cleansing". So OK, I'm finished about dat.

Screwballs. Well da kine of screwballs I mean are da ones you can buy in da store in da ice cream section eh. Dey're in a little plastic, see-through cone an dey usehually come with der own little wooden spoon, right der in da freezer, whole bunch of dem held together by elastic. An da ice cream inside is pink with da ribbons of other flavours in der eh. Mmmm. Dey're good. But you know, dey're sometimes hard to fine eh. Like on da weekend. I couldn't fine any screwballs so I ended up walkin'. An it's a beautiful day. An der's famly's out rakin' der yards. Pullin' up all dose brown leaves an makin' sure da grass is breathin' again. An I see people walkin' der dogs. An some people jus walkin'. An I walk some more an I en up near dat BDI place eh. An der's a whole bunch of people der buyin' ice cream. Boy at last I said. Here it is still pretty cold in da Manitoba an der's a bunch of people buyin' ice cream. I tink I found my screwballs. I'm jus kiddin'. I love dat us people in Manitoba is so desprate for spring to get started dat we start buyin' ice cream en of March eh. I even saw people outside on restraunt patios too eh. I guess da spring an all dat means is really here. An dat's good. I tink my favrit part is when we do da tings where we're peelin' away da stuff we doan need an showin' what's underneath, all da fresh an good stuff. Jus like da screwballs eh. I findly foun one an boy was it good. An you know, der in da bottom was da prize eh. Piece of gum. Dat's been sittin' in dat ice cream for who knows how long. You almos break yer teeth on it if yer not careful. I hope you guys fine da important tings you need in yer lives dis week. Da stuff dat's under all dat other stuff we pile on top, like work an jobs, an worryin' an gettin' stressed. Underneath all dat is somethin' real good. An maybe even join res of us screwballs who is lookin' for ice cream outside even dough der's still snow on da groun eh. I'm Joe from Winnipeg. Meegwetch.

Ian's Notes

Mouses

OK. Here's what happened. One night I bought some junk food and a really big chocolate bar. I went home and ate the junk food and placed the big chocolate bar on a small table, but it fell off. So I remember thinking, "I should pick that up. Nahhh." So I went on watching TV. The next day, I'd forgotten about the chocolate bar and was watching TV. And then I heard this noise. I can't write it. I can only make the sound. Basically do your best mouse impersonation and then go "tch tch tch" or something and that will be what it sounded like. So I turned down the TV because I thought that's what it was and it went away. So I turned the TV back up and then I heard it again. Anyways, I looked to my side and there was a little mouse eating my big chocolate bar that had fallen on the floor. I jumped up and crouched behind the side of the couch watching him. And from then on it was all out war. Me sitting in a chair by the only door he could get out with a running shoe in my hand. I was even contemplating finding a BB gun. Needless to say, I was surprised by my own over-reaction. I don't know if it was 'cause that mouse was eating my chocolate bar or if it was because he scared me. Anyways, we borrowed my dad's cat after that and the house has been mouse-free ever since. Although the cat became a whole other problem.

NSF

My picking on banks again, but they really make me mad. Just recently I deposited a cheque which they thought looked shifty and so they put a hold on the cheque. Problem was, they put a hold on all of my money in that account. Even the money that was there before and all I wanted was $20. When I tried to get satisfaction they just told me I couldn't get any money. That's when I used the toll-free number on the back of my bank card. I highly recommend it. I got results in minutes. Anyhow, banks will always be a source of material as long as they treat our money like it's theirs. Boy, I sound like a grouchy old man. I wonder how I will sound when I am a grouchy old man?

Moose on the Road

This Joe came about after I did the Joe from the western part of Manitoba, which I recorded in a hotel room over the phone. I appreciated seeing more of Manitoba than I usually do. It's a good reminder that it's a big province, and a beautiful one too. Anyways, I was on a tour of my show *fareWel*, so we were going all over the place, that's where this Joe comes from. One morning I was the only one awake and I saw what I thought was somebody walking on the road, and I was gonna pick them up to keep me company. But when they turned sideways I saw they were a moose. Oh well. This Joe was also kind of a rejuvenation for me, because after experiencing something very unpleasant with some of the cast members in western Manitoba, I was quite depressed. I was depressed because I talked about how friendly and wonderful everyone was, but unfortunately, not everyone was friendly and wonderful. But, while I was feeling depressed this big guy named Thor said "Meegwetch" to me while we were waiting for the hamburgers we ordered. And the fact that this guy made an effort and was speaking an aboriginal language made me feel great.

Plastic

Here I thought I'd leave a bit of my brain on the page. Sometimes I have too many ideas and I want to talk about all of them. That's been a lifelong problem for me if you ask my family. I often write my ideas and the Joe's in my head before I write them down. Sometimes it goes the other way, but I hope some of you are interested in the process a little bit. Maybe those of you who write yourselves or are interested in it. I'd highly recommend it. It's hard, but rewarding and it's something you're always discovering.

Who's the Boss?

Again, more of my brain. This time inside the text. I often try to construct jokes. Not very well, mind you. I like to think the humour works better if it comes out of the story I'm telling. The other way, like in this piece, just doesn't work as well. And I often leave the joke out.

Ian Ross

Ian Ross was born in McCreary, Manitoba, and calls the communities of Fairford, Kinosota and Winnipeg home. He has been writing plays for several years, and *fareWel* marked his first professional mainstage production. That play was also the winner of the 1997 Governor General's Award for Drama. His first children's play, *Baloney!*, about child poverty in Canada, was produced in the spring of 1998 by Manitoba Theatre for Young People. He continues to enjoy writing and living in Winnipeg.